Uniform with this volume
and in the same
series

THE TEACH YOURSELF BOOKS

A SHORT DICTIONARY OF
LANGUAGES

THE TEACH YOURSELF BOOKS

A SHORT DICTIONARY
OF LANGUAGES

by

D. S. PARLETT

THE ENGLISH UNIVERSITIES PRESS LTD.
ST. PAUL'S HOUSE WARWICK LANE
LONDON E.C.4

To my wife
BARBARA

———————

First Printed 1967

Copyright © 1967
The English Universities Press Ltd

SBN 340 05983 4

Printed in Great Britain for the English Universities Press, Limited
by Elliott Bros. & Yeoman Limited, Speke, Liverpool.

CONTENTS

INTRODUCTION

THE AIM of the Dictionary is to provide a certain amount of basic information—social, historical, statistical, linguistic —about a number of languages, arranged for convenience in alphabetical order. I hope it might be found useful by several groups of people: those who study or are actively concerned with linguistics, history, sociology, and indeed with the humanities in general, for all human ideas and institutions depend for their establishment and maintenance on the fact of language; those who are interested in the world about them, though not from any specialist point of view, since questions of language, e.g. the struggle of linguistic minorities, such as the Flemish speakers of Belgium, are often overtly in the news and, perhaps less obviously, underlie current events and political activities as much as they do historical, cultural and ethnological studies; and those who simply enjoy browsing through reference books.

The Dictionary of Languages does fill a gap of which, I think, many linguists are conscious. Nothing similar has been produced in English since Bonwick's *Rudimentary Dictionary of Universal Philology* (1873), now out of print and far outdated. There are, however, two works which approach the aim mentioned above. Mario Pei's *The World's Chief Languages* (Allen & Unwin, 3rd Ed. 1961) selects, as the title indicates, a number of languages of major importance throughout the world, those with which a slight but practical knowledge would enable the traveller to get about without an interpreter in whatever country he may be. The languages are not arranged alphabetically, but occupy whole chapters or parts of chapters according to the extent of their 'world significance'; the major languages are described in some detail, a condensed grammar, vocabulary, everyday phrases

and sample text being given with each. The other is a monu
mental compilation in French, *Les Langues du Monde* (ed
Meillet & Cohen, pub. C.N.R.S., Paris, 2nd ed. 1952). Th
object of this work, running to 1,294 pages and 20 map
mostly in colour, is quite simply to give a specialist surve
of all known and recorded languages: they are dealt with i
related groups, each group written by an expert in tha
particular field. The editors have avowedly imposed n
restrictions on the various writers, unless the request to b
fully comprehensive be counted as such. As a whole, there
fore, the work is complete and meticulous, but lacks unit
of approach, method and emphasis, resulting in incon
sistencies which sometimes retard rather than advanc
points of research made by reference to it. Nevertheless, i
remains a bottomless gold-mine to linguists.

The present work attempts neither to rival nor to emulat
these books; it differs in form and approach, and may
perhaps, be regarded as supplementary to them both.

Scope of the Dictionary. The number of languages a
present scattered over the globe is immense: it is generall
put at about 3,000. This gives a rough idea of the sort c
range involved, but is so imprecise as to serve little othe
useful purpose. Based on a strict definition of the term
language and excluding those forms of speech which fror
any point of view might be regarded as *dialects* of othe
languages, the number could be reduced to several hundreds
with the inclusion of carefully differentiated dialects it coul
be increased to at least 5,000.

Those selected for the Dictionary include:

(a) the languages spoken in Europe, regardless of status o
importance;

(b) languages of the INDO-EUROPEAN group, to whic
belong English and the majority of the most widesprea
languages of civilization, such as Russian, French, Spanis
etc. It should be noted that not all of the languages of Europ

belong to this group, and, conversely, that many Indo-European languages are spoken outside the European continent;

(c) such dialects of (a) and (b) as are sufficiently distinct to be definable;

(d) national languages, i.e. those which act as the official medium of administration, education, etc, in particular countries;

(e) languages spoken by minority groups in countries where the national language is of a different kind—these include for example languages indigenous to regions within the USSR, but exclude regional variants or dialects of the national language;

(f) such dialects of (d) and (e) as are sufficiently distinct to be definable;

(g) any other languages of cultural or historical significance, including many which are no longer spoken.

Excluded are *artificial* or *constructed* languages (e.g. Esperanto), and *hybrid* or *contact* languages (e.g. Pidgin English).

Entries are also included for:

(h) names of families and groups of languages mentioned in the text;

(i) alternative names of languages or their groups, where the less common titles may still be occasionally met;

(j) recognizable dialects which do not merit a distinct place but which are mentioned in a particular language entry, to which they are cross-referenced;

(k) geographical/ethnographical names which have no necessary linguistic validity but are used for convenience or the avoidance of confusion, e.g. Amerindian, African. Otherwise, purely geographical entries are avoided.

All entries are in English or anglicized form. For use of block capitals, abbreviations and symbols, see p 9.

The basic pattern of information given for each language

is given below. It should be noted, however, that (i) the amount of information varies according to the significance of the language and to the amount of consistent information available, and (ii) the pattern may be extended, curtailed or otherwise re-arranged according to circumstance.

(a) language name in English, any alternative name that may be found, and indigenous name where possible (e.g. *Deutsch* for *German*);

(b) classification to enable cross-reference to the group of which it is a representative and thence to other related languages. For explanation of the system used, see p 5.

(c) number of speakers, where known, or date of extinction, where appropriate;

(d) identity of speakers, place of origin, and extension, where appropriate;

(e) principal dialects, where distinguishable; and standard where appropriate;

(f) any historical information, which may consist only of date of earliest records or of first known description;

(g) present status, e.g. whether national language, minority language, or only in specialized use (e.g. Latin);

(h) script or scripts that may be used, and extent of literature, if any;

(i) brief description of the language, noting salient points of phonetic, lexical and grammatical structure;

(j) in many cases, the numerals from 1 to 10, and 100, (see p 7).

Entries for dialects are cross-referenced to the appropriate language entry, but may include additional information.

Entries for language groups generally include information on the essential linguistic and historical features of the group as a whole, and reference made to any larger or smaller groups that may be appropriate.

Classification. Linguists and research workers who specialize in particular languages and groups of languages are naturally concerned with the question of classification, the basis of which lies in the establishment of groups of languages which have many grammatical and lexical points in common, suggesting that they are historically related, and in relating one group to another because of more general similarities, and so on. There is at present no authoritatively established classification of languages as a whole which can be drawn on in this Dictionary without fear of contradiction. There is however a great deal of agreement amongst linguists for the classification of languages belonging to most of the major and well-established groups, such as the Indo-European languages, and in most such cases it has been possible to refer to the works of leading authorities in particular groups or to follow standard lines of classification about which there is little doubt.

The purpose of classifying, as far as the Dictionary is concerned, is to enable the reader to refer from one language to others which are similar and related to it, and to save space by describing the characteristics of individual languages under the heading of the whole group, so that within each language entry it is possible to concentrate more on historical, cultural and statistical information.

The classification is made by use of abbreviations following, in round brackets, the language name forming each entry. Each classification reference is in two parts:

(1) An abbreviation in capital letters, denoting the FAMILY to which the language belongs. 'Family' is the term generally given to a series of languages all of which are thought to be historically related, even though the similarities between individual members may at present not be apparent, and none of which bears any satisfactorily demonstrable relationship with any language not of the family. In other words, it is the largest closed group. Some languages are so

individual and distinct that no clear relationships are discernible—or generally accepted—between them and other
languages or families. In this case, as far as we are concerned, the language name serves also as a family name.
Thus Japanese is followed by the reference (JP), with no
further subdivision, and Basque by (BQ): this indicates
immediately that the languages concerned are quite distinct.
(As it happens, some linguists have suggested that Japanese
and Basque are related, but their opinion carries little weight
and there is no conclusive evidence to support the inclusion
of both within a larger family). At the other extreme, there
are large groups of languages occupying distinct—and vast
—geographic areas, such as those of Negro-Africa, in which
researches have not yet resulted in the establishment of
incontestably distinct families. In such cases, for convenience here, these are lumped together into a super-family
and distinguished by the use of three, instead of two, initials.
Thus, for example, (NAF) refers to the non-committal term
NEGRO-AFRICAN.

The Key to these abbreviations appears on page 9.

(2) An abbreviation in small letters, denoting the appropriate group within the family to which the language may
be attached. If this is a proper name (whether linguistic,
ethnic or geographical) it is given as a pair of initials, e.g.
within the family INDO-EUROPEAN (IE) we have (rm) denoting
the Romance languages, (gm) the Germanic, (sv) the
Slavonic, and so on. Any further divisions, generally
accepted, appear as a single initial, e.g. (IE/ct.b) reads INDO-
EUROPEAN/Celtic branch, Brythonic group. In some cases
the secondary division is a purely geographic reference, e.g.
(IE/ir.w) denotes the western group of the Iranian languages,
which belong to the family INDO-EUROPEAN.

**The Key to further subdivisions is to be found in the
appropriate heading entry.** E.g. suppose reference is
being made to the Irish language. The classification is given

as (IE/ct.g). The key giving (IE) =INDO-EUROPEAN is found on p. 9. The entry for INDO-EUROPEAN gives all subdivisions of that family represented in the Dictionary, from which it will be seen that (ct) = Celtic, and, in the same heading, the relation of Celtic to other language groups of Europe will be found. Reference then to the heading Celtic will show that (ct.g) denotes the Goidelic or Gaelic branch, and will also reveal linguistic and historical information about the Celtic languages as a whole. Finally, the relationship of Irish to Manx and Scots Gaelic is explained under the heading Gaelic.

Spelling and Phonetic Script

The numerals from 1 to 10 are given in many entries, and may appear in one of three forms:

(1) In normal Roman script, for languages which use this alphabet regularly. They are written as they usually appear in print, i.e. following the correct orthography, which is unlikely to be phonetically accurate.

(2) In *italics*, for languages which do not normally use the Roman alphabet but which are regularly transliterated. The form given is the usual transliterated form. Cyrillic script (for Slavonic languages mainly) is now customarily transliterated with use of *č* and *š* for *ch* (*tch*) and *sh* (*sch*), *t'* and *p'* for palatalized variants of *t* and *p* etc.

(3) In phonetics, indicated by appearing between square brackets: [ ]. Each symbol has one value only, indicated below.
Consonants
[p t k b d g f v s z m n l r h]: approximately as in English, with *g* and *s* hard.
[q]: like *k*, articulated further back (unvoiced uvular plosive);
[č]: like *ch* in *church*;
[ć]: midway between [t^s] and [č];
[ç]: like *ch* in German *ich*;

[x]: like *ch* in Scottish *loch*, German *ach*;

[X]: like [x], but articulated further back (unvoiced uvular fricative);

[ħ]: like [χ], but still further back; energetic form of *h*;

[ʔ]: glottal stop, as in Cockney *bo'l* for *bottle*;

[ɟ]: like *j* and *dg* in *judge*; voiced version of [č];

[ʕ]: voiced variety of [ħ];

[š]: like *sh* in *shed*;

[ž]: like *s* in *measure*, *j* in French *je*;

[ŝ]: midway between [s] and [ž];

[θ]: like *th* in *thick*;

[ð]: like *th* in *then*;

[R]: uvular *r*, as used in French;

[ŋ]: like *ng* in *singing* (not as in *finger*, this would be-[ŋg]);

[ɲ]: = [nj], i.e. *ni* as in *onion*, or the *ñ* of Spanish *señor*.

[ḍ] [ṇ]: etc, are retroflex varieties of [d] [n], etc;

[tʲ]: represents palatalized [t], i.e. slightly coloured by [j]; also [tˢ] indicates [t] coloured by [s], rather like the sound written in German as *z*; similarly [pʲ tʰ pʰ], etc.

Semi-vowels

[w]: like *w* in *wet*; [j] like *y* in *yet*.

Vowels

[i e a o u] represent the pure vowel sounds of e.g. Italian, Spanish;

[ä]: as *ä* in German *älter*; slightly more closed than the *e* of English *get*;

[ö]: as in German *öde*, like *eu* in French *peu*; more closed than the *ir* of *bird*;

[ü]: as German *ü*; as French *u* in *tu*;

[å]: as in Swedish *å*; similar to *o* in *got*;

[ị]: *i* with tongue lowered, as in Slavonic;

[ə]: neutral or unclear *e*, like that of *butter*.

Vowel modifications

[ō]: long vowel;   [ŏ]: short vowel;

[ǫ]: open vowel;   [ọ]: closed vowel.

Abbreviations and Symbols used in Text

(1) Classificatory abbreviations: language families in SMALL CAPITALS, unrelated and unclassifiable languages in lower case:

AB: AUSTRALIAN ABORIGINE	**IE**: INDO-EUROPEAN
AL: ALTAIC	**JP**: Japanese
AN: Andaman	**KR**: Korean
AS: AUSTRO-ASIAN	**MP**: MALAYO-POLYNESIAN
BQ: Basque	**NH**: Nahali
BR: Burushaski	**PP**: PAPUAN
CC: CAUCASIAN	**PS**: PALAEO-SIBERIAN
DV: DRAVIDIAN	**SN**: SINITIC
HS: HAMITO-SEMITIC	**UR**: URALIAN

(2) Symbols and other abbreviations:

L, LL: Language, languages;

D, DD: Dialect, dialects;

C, CC: Century (**C8AD** = 8th Cent. A.D., **CC3-4BC** = 3rd to 4th Cents. B.C.);

c: Approximately;

m: Million(s);

th: Thousand(s);

L^x: Extinct language (e.g. Cornish^x);

L*: Liturgical or other 'special' language (e.g. Latin*);

L^o: Empty language, i.e. a series of closely related dialects lacking a literary or other formal standard (e.g. Kurdish^o);

=: Synonymous with, equivalent to, signifies;

≠: Distinct from, not to be confused with.

9

ABBREVIATIONS

(3) Sample entry showing use of abbreviations:

Ukrainian (Ruthenian, Ukraïnskij): (IE/sv.e) 37 m; (etc). Two bracketed names represent respectively alternative name, and the indigenous name of the language. IE = INDO-EUROPEAN family (see above). Reference to that entry reveals *sv* = Slavonic branch; reference to latter entry reveals *e* = Eastern group, and shows relationship of Ukrainian to other Slavonic languages. 37 m = 37 million speakers.

A SHORT DICTIONARY OF
LANGUAGES

A

Abkaz (Abkhaz)

(CC.N/nw) 70 th in Abkhaz ASSR. Some literature from end C19 in Cyrillic script; post-revolutionary publications in Roman. Typically complex Caucasian language, having no fewer than 75 distinct sounds.

Aborigine

see AUSTRALIAN.

Adyge

(CC.N/nw) 252 th (in 1939) in Adygey autonomous region. DD Cherkessian & Kabardin. Has literary status, using modified Roman alphabet.

Afar (Dankali)

(HS/cs.c) Minor language of N.E. Ethiopia.

Afghan

see Pushto.

Afrikaans

(IE/gm.w) Since 1925 the official language of South Africa, though less extensive than English. Basically Dutch (whose 13 m speakers include those of Afrikaans) with which it is mutually intelligible. The vocabulary is almost entirely Dutch, though with some English loan-words (e.g. *moter-kar*) and simplified spelling. Grammar also simplified in some respects, e.g. coalescence of Common and Neuter genders. Numerals: een twee drie vier vyf ses sewe ag(t) nege tien (Compare Dutch).

Agaw

(HS/cs.c) Cushitic language of N. Ethiopia, region of Lake Tana. Now giving way to Amharic, qv. Numerals: [lag ləŋa siχwa saǰǰa ankuā waltā laŋata soχwata sassā čəka, lēn = 100].

Aimak

D of Mongolian, qv.

Ainu

?(PS) 1.5 th (in 1935). The Ainu tribes of the South Sakhalin seem to represent earlier invaders of the region than the Japanese. Simple phonetic system, loosely agglutinative in structure, with loans and influences from Palaeosiberian and Japanese; not satisfactorily classifiable. Numerals: [šine tu re ine ašik īwan aruwan tupesan šinepesan wan] 100 = [tanku] (loan word from Tungusic).

Albanian (Shqipeja)

(IE/al) 1.9 m in Albania; small colonies of Albanian speakers in USA, Greece, Italy. DD: Geg (north of Shkumbini), Tosk (south); the Standard is Geg. The rather mysterious language of Albania, unrecorded before C15, was recognized as Indo-European in C19 but is not closely related to any of the other branches. Possibly a descendant of Illyrian[x], qv. Folk-songs and tales collected in C19; now written in Roman script but Tosk dialect formerly in Greek. Grammar more archaic than most IE languages; much vocabulary seems borrowed from Latin. Numerals: një dy tre katër pesë gjashtë shtatë tetë nëntë dhjetë; 100 qint. (ë = [ə]. Compare Latin, Greek, Sanskrit). *Nothing about Kosmet.*

Alentejano

D of Portuguese, qv.

Algarvio

D of Portuguese, qv.

Altaic

(AL) Family consisting of the Turkic, Mongolian and Tungusic language groups, qqv, which together cover most of Asia. Each group is very homogeneous, showing dialectal variation which, having regard to the vast area covered by these languages, is very slight. Though generally accepted, however, the genealogical relationship of these three groups is not fully established. All three show remarkable correspondences in phonetics, vocabulary and syntax which suggest relationship, but many may be to a large extent due to borrowings and mutual influences, since the languages concerned are for the most part spoken by nomadic tribes and thus remain free from the restraining effects of administrative and literary usage. All are basically agglutinative in structure and given to vowel harmony, in varying degrees. This again suggests a basic relationship, but both features are to be found also in the Uralian languages. This has led some to speak of a combined URAL-ALTAIC family, but until much more work has been done in describing and classifying the Altaic languages so that sufficient comparison becomes possible this must remain hypothetical. Some attach Japanese, Korean, and even Ainu to the Altaic family.

AL/tk: Turkic (Turkish, Chuvash, Yakut, etc)
AL/mg: Mongolian (Buryat, Khalka, Kalmyk, etc)
AL/tg: Tungusic (Tungus, Lamut, Manchu)

For examples of vowel harmony, see Turkish.

Amerindian

(AMR), Languages of the original inhabitants of the American continent number over a thousand. Today the remaining languages of North America, from Eskimo to Nahuatl, are spoken by perhaps a few hundred thousand people. Before colonization this vast area was very sparsely populated, mainly by nomadic tribes, resulting in extreme diversification of dialects, languages and major groups, so that linguists are unable to group them satisfactorily into distinct families. Six major Stocks or 'superfamilies' are sometimes reckoned for convenience: (1) Algonkin-Wakash (Cree, Shawnee, Cheyenne, etc); (2) Eskimo-Aleut; (3) Hoka-Sioux (Mohawk, Cherokee, Siouan etc); (4) Na-Dene

(Chippeway, Navaho, Apache); (5) Penutia (Chinook, etc); (6) Uto-Aztec-Tano (Shoshone, Comanche, Nahuatl).

South America has several million speakers of native languages; these have been only slightly studied—many have yet to be discovered—and offer great scope for linguistic exploration. Some have profited by the introduction of Spanish and Portuguese by acquiring loan-words, and some are actually increasing in number of speakers. However, Amerindian languages in general are insignificant except from a linguistic viewpoint, and their extinction is only a matter of time.

Amharic

(HS/eo) 3–5 m The only officially recognized language of Ethiopia (but see Ethiopic); in Amhara and large areas of central Ethiopia, and boasting second to Arabic the greatest numbers of speakers amongst the Semitic languages. Literature from C14; today, as it gains in ascendancy over its neighbours, Amharic is used more for administrative and press purposes than for creative literature. The name Amharic refers also to its alphabet.

Andaman

(AN) Aboriginal language of the Andaman islands, spoken by only 460 people in 1931. Thoroughly investigated, but unrepresented in historical records and cannot be satisfactorily related to any other language group. Numerals: [ūba tūl] = 1, [ĭkpōr] = 2 or 'several', [dōgā] = many, the whole, the lot.

Anglo-Saxon[x]

(IE/gm.w) Old English, see English. For other 'Saxon' terms, see Saxon.

Annamese (Annamite)

?(SN/th) or (AS) 14 m, Vietnam. Negligible indigenous literature, Chinese being formerly used for this purpose, though some records of Annamese in Chinese characters. Roman alphabet, introduced by missionaries in C17. Either a Thai type Sinitic language with strong influence of Mon-Khmer, or vice-versa.

Arabic

(HS/ab) 75 m, ranging from west coast of Africa to east coast of greater Arabia. DD (1) in Saudi Arabia etc: Arabic proper, Hijaz, Hejd, Najd, Yemenese, Datinese, Omanese, Shahi; (2) to the north: Iraqian, Syro-Palestinian, Lebanese; (3) to the west: Egyptian (≠ Egyptian language, qv), Shuwa, Maltese (by 2 th Christian Maltese and written in Roman script), Lybian, Tripolitan, Tunisian, Algerian, Andalusian (Hispanic), Moroccan, Hassani. Other DD, extinct, also recorded. Distinct from South Arabic, qv.

Earliest inscription 328AD at En Nemara; Arabic alphabet first appears 512 AD. A rich and flourishing literature from its earliest appearance includes scientific, poetic, secular and religious works. The Koran dates from C7, since when Arabic has been the evangelizing medium of Islam.

Great cultural and therefore linguistic influence on the Western world, especially through Spanish as a result of the Moorish invasions (C5AD). The Spanish definite article *el* is influenced by Arabic *al*, which is also to be seen in e.g. *alcohol* (> *al* + *koh'l*, a very fine powder), algebra (> *al* + *jebr*, a setting or re-union), *alkali* (> *al* + *qali*, ashes of salt-wort).

Dialectal differentiation not very great: the standard Modern Arabic, as used by the press throughout the Arabic-speaking world, is in fact the very conservative classical form of the language, from which the vernaculars differ in varying degrees.

In form it is most typical of the Semitic languages (qv for description), the tri-literal roots being very clearly marked in the classical language. Noun distinguishes masculine/

feminine, definite/indefinite, three cases, and three numbers, including dual. Adjective follows and agrees. Verb has three main conjugations: perfect denoting actions regarded as complete, imperfect denoting actions regarded as continuous, and imperative. No tenses as such: time denoted by adverbs. Personal suffixes to verbs and prepositions.

Numerals (spoken Egyptian; the ending —a is dropped before feminine nouns and vowels), transliterated: *wâhid 'itnen talâta 'arba'a khamsa sitta saba'a tamanya tis'a 'ashara*, 100 = *miyya*. Iraqi has 2 *'ithnen*, 3 *thalath*, 8 *thaman*. Phonetics: [ʔāħid ʔitnēn, (ʔiθnēn) talāt(a), (θalaθ) ʔarbaʕ(a) χams(a) sitt(a) sabaʕ(a) taman(ja), (θaman) tisʔ(a) ʕašar(a), 100 = mijja]. (Compare Hebrew.) Attention has often been drawn to the similarity of Arabic (and related) numerals *sitta*, *saba'a* to those of Indo-European languages, cf *six, seven*.

Aramaic

(HS/nw) 200 th speakers in three areas: (1) border of Iraq/Iran, south of Lake Urmia; (2) western Syria, near the coast; (3) border of Syria/Turkey.

First appears C8BC. Aramaic secretaries were employed in the administration of the ancient Akkadian empire, and it achieved importance as a language of officialdom. Overcame Hebrew, Phoenician and Akkadian, also Greek in Asia but gave way to it on the Mediterranean coast; flourished CC7—3BC. The language of Christ, it was at that time widespread over the whole of Palestine and present-day Iraq; its speakers never constituted a unified national state, however, and it is now considerably on the decline.

Aranda (Aranta, Arunta)

see AUSTRALIAN Aborigine.

Argobba

(HS/eo) 2 th in Ethiopia, small patch east of Shoa, south of Harar. Fast declining in favour of Amharic.

Armenian (Hahyeren)

(IE/ar) 3·5 m in Armenian SSR, parts of Georgian SSR, Azerbaijan and Iran. Dialects very diversified. An independent and distinct member of the Indo-European languages, geographically and linguistically midway between European branches (Greek, Slavonic) and their Indian cousins (Iranian, Indo-Aryan).

Reduced to writing by Christian Church in C5. Old literary standard, *Grabar*, used by scholars until C19, and still the liturgical language of the Armenian Church. The name Armenian refers also to its alphabet. Influences mainly from Persian, but also from Caucasian, Greek (through Christianity) and French (through the Crusades). Numerals: *meg y-ergu y-erek chors hinq vets yo't'n vutn inn dasn*; 100 = *hariur*.

Aryan

= INDO-EUROPEAN, qv. (≠ Indo-Aryan LL, qv).

Asianic

Geographical term of convenience, referring to the extinct LL of Asia Minor and the Mediterranean region which do not belong to known groups. Entries for Etruscan[x] and Sumerian[x].

Ashkun

D of Kafir[o], qv.

Assamese

(IE/ia.e) 2 m in Brahmaputra valley, north-east of East Pakistan. Has a lengthy literary background.

Asuri

D of Bhili[o], qv.

Australian (Aborigine)

(AB) The native languages of Australia, spoken by hunting

and food-gathering tribes over the greater part of the continent, are dying out without any overall detailed description or classification, though some individual languages, such as Aranda and Worora, have been quite fully examined. It is quite certain that all can be grouped in one major genealogical family; the most detailed classification on a grammatical basis is that of Capell (1937) who distinguishes five major groups. Despite some similarities, no relationship has been shown with Papuan or Polynesian languages. Numerals (Aranda): [ɲinta] = 1, [tara] = 2, [urbutʲa] = 3 or 'a few'; most languages stop here, but Aranda and some others construct numbers a little further: [taramanaɲinta] = 3, [taramatara] = 4, [taramataramaɲinta] = 5, literally 'two and two and one'.

Austro-Asian (AS)

An ill-defined family consisting of two major language groups and a few languages difficult to classify, found in south-east Asia. The grouping below is not universally accepted, and no positive genealogical relationship has been demonstrated. AUSTRO-ASIAN or AUSTRO-ASIATIC may also be found as a group including these and the SINITIC languages, and AUSTRIC as a term relating them with MALAYO-POLYNESIAN languages.

(1) Mon-Khmer LL of Indo-China;

(2) Munda or Kolarian LL of India;

(3) Possibly Annamese, which may however be SINITIC; possibly Cham, which may be MALAYO-POLYNESIAN.

Austromelanesian

see MALAYO-POLYNESIAN.

Austronesian

= MALAYO-POLYNESIAN, qv.

Avar (Awar)

(CC.N/e) 159 th (in 1926); Caucasian language of Daghestan. Arabic script introduced, C19, but since the Revolution a modified Roman script is used for educational purposes.

Avestan[x]
(IE/ir.e) Language of the Avesta, holy book of Zoroastranism, still the religion of the Parsees (Persians). Closely related to Old Persian; extinct since C6BC.

Awadhi
D of Hindi (East), qv.

Azerbaijani (Azerbaichani)
(AL/tk) 3·5 m (in 1959). An important language of the Caucasus, extending also into Iran. Abundant literature, especially drama, since C16. Latin alphabet introduced 1922, later replaced by Cyrillic.

B

Badaga
(DV) 30 th speakers in mountainous region east of Mangalore, India.

Bagheli
D of Hindi (East), qv.

Balti
The standard D of Tibetan, qv.

Baltic LL
(IE/bt) These consist of Lithuanian, Latvian (Lettish), and Old Prussian.[x] They are Indo-European languages, sometimes grouped with Slavonic: the two groups share many features distinguishing them from other IE languages, but similarities may be largely due to a parallel evolution rather than to a very close genetic relationship. These

languages show archaic Indo-European traits, particularly Lithuanian. ($\neq$ Baltic Fennic, below).

Baltic Fennic LL

(UR/fn.b) A Branch of URALIAN, qv, consisting of Finnish (Suomi, Karelian & Olonecian); Vepsian, Ludian, Votian; Estonian and Livonian.

Balto-Slavonic LL

see Baltic LL.

Baluchi

(IE/ir. w) 225 th in West Pakistan. 2 dialects, North and South fairly distinct and separated by an isolated pocket of Brahui, an Indo-Aryan language. Oral literature only.

Bangaru

D of Hindi (West), qv.

Bantu

(NAF) The Bantu languages, of which Swahili is the best-known member, occupy most of Africa from the Equator southwards and have long been recognized as a linguistically coherent group, but the exact position of this group in regard to other Negro African tongues is not satisfactorily determined. Traditionally, Bantu has been treated as a distinct family and contrasted with a 'Sudanic' family ranging from Senegal to Somalia, but it seems more closely related to the western Sudanic LL than do the eastern Sudanic LL themselves. Typical of all Bantu languages is the feature of noun-classes, for examples of which see Swahili.

Bashgali

D of Kafir⁰, qv.

Bashkir

(AL/tk) A Turkic language spoken in the Bashkir SSR, sometimes regarded as a D of Volga Tartar.

Basque (Euskara)

(BQ) 700 th around the south-east coastal angle of the Bay of Biscay, straddling the Western Pyrenees; 80% in Spain, 20% France. Extensive dialectal differentiation.

Its origin and affinities are unknown. Some have held it to be the last remnant of unrecorded Iberian LL spoken in the Hispanic peninsula before Roman occupation, others a member of a hypothetical 'Mediterranean' family including Etruscan[x] and Caucasian, and yet others have sought to relate it to Japanese and North American languages. Most likely possibility is the relationship with CAUCASIAN, qv. Evidently once more extensive: the name *Gascony* cognate with *Basque*. Cf tribe *Vascones* in Roman times.

Texts from C16 mainly religious until C19, since when there has been a great advance in scope and quantity of literary productions.

Agglutinative structure. Verb complicated through being intransitive in use (e.g. not '*I eat food*' but '*by me food is eaten*') and incorporation of 'subject' and 'object' pronouns. Much borrowing from Romance and Celtic LL, and Arabic. Numerals: bat bi hirur laur bortz sei zazpi zortzi bederatzi hamar; 100 = ehun (probably from Germanic through Vandal and Visigoth conquests, C5AD).

Baxtiyari

D of Persian, qv.

Beirão

D of Portuguese, qv.

Beja

(HS/cs.c) Language of northern Ethiopia, spoken by tribes Bishari, Hadendoa, Halenga, Ben-Amer. Now giving way to Arabic, but flourishing in C19.

Bengali

(IE/ia.e) 65 m in delta of the Ganges, including Calcutta

and East Pakistan. Literature of long standing, includes
the writings of Rabindranath Tagore. Borrowings from
Sanskrit and Hindi.

Berber

(HS/bb) Probably over 4 m speakers, both settled and
nomadic, in North Africa including the Sahara. Dialects
uniform grammatically, but wide variation in accent and
pronunciation may render some of them mutually unintelligible: Tuareg (Sahara, inc. Timbuctu, Zinder, Ghat);
Shluh, Beraber, Rifian (Morocco, from south to north);
Zenaga (Mauritania); Kabyle (Algeria); Zenatian (loose
term to denote other DD of Algeria and patches to the east).
The extinct Guancha of the Canary Islands was probably
also of this type.

The Berbers represent a distinct ethnic and linguistic
type, once spread in a coherent group over the whole of
North Africa (C5BC). Numerous documents, in Arabic
script, from C12AD. Numerals (Tuareg): [jən sin kərað
okkoz səmmus sədis əssaa əttam təzzaa məraw], 100 =
[timiði].

Bhili⁰

(IE/ia.w) 2 m speakers of the Bhili dialects in central
India. DD: Kharia, Asuri, Korwa, Ho, Bhumij, Mundari,
Santali.

Bhili

(DV) Minor Dravidian dialect in western India, practically extinct.

Bhojpuri

D of Bihari, qv.

Bhumij

D of Bhili⁰, qv.

Bihari

(IE/ia.e) 35 m in Magadha, N.E. India. DD: Maithili, Magahi, Bhojpuri. Literature of long standing, mainly in Maithili dialect.

Bokmål

= Norwegian, qv.

Brahui

(DV) 200 th speakers of a Dravidian language situated away from the main body of Dravidian as an isolated pocket in S.E. Iran (suggesting that Dravidian may have been formerly widespread to this extent). Surrounded on all sides by Iranian languages.

Braj

D of Hindi (West), qv.

Breton (Breiz, Brezonek)

(IE/ct.b) 750th, Brittany, speakers bilingual with French. DD Léonais or Léonard (of S. Pol de Léon; the purest and principal dialect); Cornouaillais (of Quimper); Trégorais or Trécorrois (of Tréguier); Vannetais (of Vannes; the most aberrant and distinctive dialect).

Represents a development of the British language brought across from Cornwall CC4-5AD before its differentiation into Breton, Cornish, Welsh. Literature, mainly religious, since C16. Numerals: un daou trî péder pemp c'houéc'h seic'h eiz naô dég, 100 = kant (Compare Welsh, Cornish).

Brythonic LL (Brittonic, British)

(IE/ct) = Welsh, Breton and Cornish[x], see Celtic LL.

Bulgarian (Bulgarski)

(IE/sv.s) 8 m, Bulgaria, with enclaves in USSR and part of Rumania. DD: the language is very homogeneous, and DD are difficult to differentiate—possibly three distinguishable, of the West, of North-east, of South-east.

Old Bulgarian (CC9–11), the language of the Slavs of Macedonia, is simply equivalent to Old or Church Slavonic (see Slavonic LL). Middle Bulgarian (CC12–16), period of subjugation of Slavs to Byzantium, during which many modern characteristics developed. Modern Bulgarian from C16; grammar appeared 1835. Russian extensively borrowed from in C19. Dictionary, 1904.

Bulgarian, though retaining three genders, has lost many inflexions and shows a tendency towards analytic constructions—cases virtually reduced to nominative and oblique (= accusative, prepositional), so prepositions in greater use. Verbal conjugation has, however, been elaborated; development of 'renarration' or 'indirect mood' for events not witnessed by the speaker. Cyrillic script. Numerals: *edin dva tri četiri pet šest sedem osem devet deset*, 100 = *sto* (Compare Russian, Polish). See also Macedonian.

Bundeli
D of Hindi (West), qv.

Burmese
(SN/tb) 10 m Burma. Some literature, but not so ancient as that of its relative Tibetan. See Tibeto-Burmese and sinitic. Numerals: [tać hnać sum le ŋa kʰrok kʰuhnać hrać ko čʰaj], 100 = [ra].

Burushaski
(BR) Language peculiar to 20 th Burusho in the Karakoram mountains of N.W. India. DD: Burushask proper in Hunza and Nagir regions, Werchikwar to the west, in Yasin. Both remain unwritten. Origins unknown cannot be related to any other language group. Numerals: [hi ālt īsk wālt tˢundo mišin tal āltam hunt tŏrm] 100 = [tʰa].

Buryat
D of Mongolian, qv.

Bushman
    see KHOIN.

Byelo-Russian (Byelorússkiy; White Russian)
    (IE/sv.e) 7 m in Byelo-Russian SSR. Sufficiently distinct from Russian to be regarded as a separate language, but considerably overshadowed by it. DD: standard is that of the south west, which is similar to the northern DD of Ukrainian. In the north east, two DD form a transition between Byelo-Russian and the northern and southern DD of Russian.

Lithuanian domination from 1315, but the Lithuanians, less civilized than the Slavs, used as language of literature and administration 'West Russian'—perhaps basically Byelo-Russian with an admixture of Ukrainian, but these and (Great) Russian were at this time little distinguished from one another. Union of Lithuania and Poland in 1569 brought greater Ukrainian influence, since Orthodox Church organized Byelo-Russian and Ukrainian lands together—in liturgy, the Ukrainian pronunciation of Church Slavonic was used. Great Polish influence from end C16. Modern literature from early C19. The 1905 revolution led to the growth of a nationalist movement, resulting in consolidation of the language and the first reliable grammar, in 1918. Byelo-Russians united in one state for the first time in 1939.

Cyrillic script. Numerals: *edzin dva try čatyry pjac' šesc' sjem vosjem dzjevjac' dzjesjac'*, 100 = *sto* (cf Church Slavonic, Russian).

C

Cambodian (Cambogian; Khmer)
    (AS/mk) 2·5 m, Cambodia. Inscriptions from C7AD.

Numerals: [muj pir bei buon prăm prăm.muj prăm.pŭl prăm.bei prăm.buon dăp] 100 = [roj] (> Siamese [roi]).

Canarese (Kanarese; Canadese)

(DV) 16 m in region of Mysore, S.W. India. Oldest inscriptions C5AD; earliest known literature an *ars poetica* of C9.

Cantonese

D of Chinese, qv.

Carelian

= Karelian, qv.

Catalan (Català)

(IE/rm.h) 5 m speakers distributed as follows: (1) Andorra, where it is the official language though French and Spanish are current; (2) France, Eastern Pyrenees (Roussillon), cultural centre Perpignan, speakers bi-lingual with French; (3) Spain, cultural centre Barcelona, speakers bi-lingual with Spanish; (4) Balearic Islands, and small colonies in Sardinia and Italy. Slight dialectal division between East and West forms.

Earliest record 1171 *Homilies d'Organyà*. One of the major European languages during the Middle Ages, standardized under James I, it was in wide use over the Mediterranean region due to extensive maritime activities of the Catalans. Major works in prose, since Provençal was the great language of poetry and was used even by Catalan poets. What were probably the first scientific and philosophical works to be written in a Romance language were those of the Catalan Ramon Llull (C13). Golden Age was C15, after which it declined until its revival in C18 as a literary medium. Repressed during the Civil War, it is slowly recovering. Numerals: un dos tres quatre cinc sis set vuit nou deu; 100 = cent. (Compare French & Spanish).

Caucasian

(CC.N & CC.S) The languages of the Caucasus, lying between the Black and the Caspian seas at extreme south-east corner of Europe in autonomous Soviet states, consist of two distinct families: North Caucasian (CC.N), and South Caucasian (CC.S) or 'Iverian'.

It is probable that the two groups are related, but not demonstrably so; as a whole they are quite distinct from Indo-European and other major language families, but it is possible that they may be connected with Basque, qv. There are similarities of structure between Basque and North Caucasian, and of vocabulary between North and South Caucasian. North and South share an extremely rich consonant system—a feature which, however, is lacking in Basque. The Caucasian languages are holding their own, owing to Soviet policy of encouraging linguistic and cultural minorities, and Russian shows no sign of ousting them: Georgian (CC.S), in fact, is the official medium of instruction in the University of Tiflis.

NORTH CAUCASIAN: two branches, East and West. East LL.: Avar, Dargwa, Chechenian; typified by complex noun system including division into 'classes'. West LL: Adyge, Abkaz; complex verb system, no noun classes (except as an independent development in Abkaz). Both groups have intransitive verbal constructions only (as Basque, qv).

SOUTH CAUCASIAN (Iverian): Georgian (Kartvelian), Mingrelian, Laz (Chan), sometimes collectively termed Zan as distinct from fourth main language: Svan.

Celtic LL

(IE/ct) These languages spread during the first millennium BC as the Celtic tribes expanded through Europe, mainly westwards (though one branch founded the kingdom of Galatia), and at the time of the Roman Empire occupied the whole of Gaul and parts of the Iberian peninsula.

They are now confined to the extreme western borders of Europe. What can be deduced of Common or Proto-Celtic indicates a close relation with the Italic languages, though the relationships are now heavily disguised. Three main groups:

(1) Gaulish[x]: the language of the ancient Gauls is imperfectly known from a few inscriptions, and became extinct in favour of Latin during C3, under Roman occupation. It appears to have been of 'p-Celtic' type and was probably very similar to the British spoken under Roman occupation.

(2) Brythonic (Brittonic): = Welsh, Breton and Cornish[x], and the language of the 'ancient' Britons, from which these are descended. Unlike Gaulish, Brythonic survived Roman occupation and the Latin language; it was the Saxons in C5 who forced Brythonic speakers westwards into Cumbria, Wales and Cornwall, and from Cornwall into Armorica (Brittany), and from that time that the division into Welsh, Cornish and Breton dates. (There appears also to have been a Cumbric variety, extinct by C12, which may have been a dialect of Welsh). Brythonic is characterized by the transformation of original Indo-European *qu* into *p* (hence the term 'p-Celtic'); thus Cornish *pymp* = *five*, of Latin *quinque*, Welsh *pwy* = *who*, cf Latin *qui(s)*.

(3) Goidelic (Gaelic): = Irish, Scots Gaelic and Manx[x], and the original Gaelic tongue from which these are derived. The Scots was differentiated from the Irish vernacular by the end of C10, and Manx from Scots shortly afterwards. Goidelic is characterized by the retention of original Indo-European *qu* (now *c*), thus Irish *cuig* = *five*, cf Latin *quinque*; Scots *co* = *who*, cf Latin *qui(s)*. Hence the term 'q-Celtic' for these languages.

Inscriptions from Scotland termed 'Pictish' are not now thought to be of Celtic provenance.

Celtic as a whole displays the feature of consonant mutation, whereby the initial consonant of a noun varies according to phonetic and grammatical context. So, e.g. Welsh *tad* = *father* may appear as *dad*, *nhad*, or *thad*; Irish *fuil* = *blood* may appear as *bhfuil*.

Cham
?(AS) 120 th speakers in the south of Indo-china of a language which some hold to be of Indonesian type.

Chan
= Laz, qv.

Chechenian
(CC.N/e) 319 th (in 1926), Caucasian language of autonomous territory of Chechniya. DD Highland and Lowland. Originally in Arabic script, changed to Roman in 1926. Some post-revolutionary literature.

Cheremissian (Mari)
(UR/fn.v) 425 th in Cheremissian SSR and Bashkir SSR.

Cherkessian (Circassian)
see Adyge.

Chhatisgarhi
D of Hindi (East), qv.

Chinese
(SN/ch) 750 m, mainly in the Chinese Republic, but 250 th in Western hemisphere and 8 m elsewhere. Of all modern living languages Chinese may boast the greatest number of speakers and the longest attested history.

The Chinese language represents a perpetual struggle between unity and diversity—unity through a continued national, cultural, political and linguistic identity, diversity due largely to the great extent of the linguistic area and to periodic shifts of imperial centres or capitals.

The most noticeable feature is the great diversity of dialects and dialectal variants, which are to a large extent mutually unintelligible. Major groups: (1) Northern Chinese, including Mandarin, Pekingese, Chin—since Pekingese is the Standard, it is difficult to number the speakers of Northern varieties; (2) Cantonese (60 m), including Sze-yap, in the Kwang-tung area; (3) Wu (50 m), including Suchow, in the region of the Yang-tse delta; (4) Min (Fukien) (50 m), including the dialects of Fuchow, Amoy, and the aberrant Hainanese; (5) Hakka (25 m) from Fukien to Kwangsi; (6) Minchia, including Lamajen, in the town of Tali in Yunnan and the surrounding plain, which is considerably divergent and was formerly thought to be non-Chinese.

By contrast, the next significant feature is the unity of the written language. The written Standard, or *Wen-li* (= 'beautiful writing'), consists of several thousand distinct characters (40 thousand possible, 4 thousand minimum essential) each of which, used singly or in compounds, is an ideograph—i.e. the character represents an idea or meaning, and not a particular set of sounds, so that speakers of mutually unintelligible dialects may read and understand the written language, unconsciously associating them with the particular forms of their own dialect. (The sentence "$4 + 7 = 11$" consists of four simple and one compound ideographs, and would be understood by a Spaniard and a Swede, though each would say it differently). The written language has thus always been of great importance in the study of Chinese as a whole.

The spoken Standard has been since 1917 the dialect of Peking, which has been formalized and, as the *Kuo-yü* (= 'national language'), is being taught throughout the Republic. At present it is supposed to be in use by about 2/3 of the population. It flourishes in areas of great dialectal diversity, such as Fukien, but in others where a *lingua franca* is already widespread—such as Cantonese in the Kwang provinces—it is still little more than another subject on the school curriculum. Ideographic writing is retained. Several methods of transliteration into Roman script are available, and late in 1966 another was adopted officially by the Chinese government.

The third characteristic of Chinese is its long standing linguistic independence: it is one of the most self-sufficient and historically pure languages of civilization. This is due only partly to the fact that its geographical position has remained constant (with extensions of boundary) through four millennia. That very few foreign word borrowings have occurred are due to the facts that (1) for most of its history Chinese culture has been superior to that of its neighbours, so the tendency to borrow has been minimal; (2) its phonetic poverty makes the assimilation of foreign elements difficult; (3) its immense background of classical vocabulary, to be drawn on as Western languages draw on Greek and Latin, has rendered loans unnecessary; (4) word borrowing entails the invention of new written characters to add to an already gigantic stock. Conversely Chinese has contributed practically nothing to Western languages during recent centuries of contact, because (1) its distinctive phonetic system is incompatible with those of Western languages (Chinese is not easily 'picked up' by Europeans), and (2) by the time contact was established, the West was sufficiently civilized to be in no need of new elements. Chinese has given the West the words 'tea' and 'cha' (same meaning, different dialects); but even such words as 'mandarin', 'pagoda', 'junk' come from other languages, such as Malay and Portuguese.

The major linguistic features of Chinese, shared with other Sinitic languages (qv) are (1) monosyllabic basis, (2) significant tonality, (3) use of classifiers with numerals. (1) All Chinese word-roots are basically monosyllabic, but the modern language has many compounds (cf English *cup-board*, *break-fast*) whose constituents, unlike these

English examples, are no longer recognizable as separate words. (2) Since roots are monosyllabic, and there are very few distinct sounds, Chinese is rich in homonyms. The consequent tendency to ambiguity of meaning is partly offset by significant tonality, i.e. words phonetically alike are distinguished by the tone of voice in which they are pronounced. Standard Pekingese theoretically distinguishes four tones; some dialects have six. (3) For use of classifiers, see example under entry SINITIC.

A rich literature is known from cC18–12BC. During the Tang dynasty, CC7–10AD, the literary language achieved a perfection not since surpassed: this form of the language is still persistent in literature, and is in any case not far removed from some of the modern dialects.

Numerals (tones not indicated): [ī erh san sᶻə wu liu či pa čiu ši] 100 = [pai].

Chude

= Vepsian, qv.

Chukchee (Luoravetlan)

(PS/ch) 12 th (in 1926) in extreme N.E. Siberia, Krai region, by largely nomadic tribes in the west and settled in the extreme east: no dialectal divergences, and probably mutually intelligible with Koryak, qv. The first book in Chukchee was published in 1932, since when slight literature has been mainly political.

Chukotian LL

= a group of PALAEOSIBERIAN languages as follows:
PS/ch.c Chukchee (Luoravetlan);
PS/ch.k Koryak (Nymylan);
PS/ch.i Kamchadal (Itelmen).

Church Slavonic★

(1) Old Church Slavonic, sometimes confusingly termed 'Old Bulgarian', or 'Old Slovenian', refers to the common

language of the Slavs of CC9–10AD before its break-up into the Russian, Polish and Serbian groups of the present day. A translation of the Bible into O. Slavonic was based on the dialect of region of Salonika, early C9, which slowly spread over the Slavonic-speaking world and produced local variants.

(2) Church Slavonic refers to the classical Slavonic language in direct lineage from O.Ch.Slav. after the development of the Slavonic LL (qv) as we now know them, which was completed by C12. It perseveres firstly as a liturgical language, in several varieties, used by Greek Orthodox Slavs, and Greek and Croatian Catholics, and secondly as a classical model to the modern languages—it served as such for example in the fixing of standard Russian in C18.

Features: Noun distinguished 3 genders (m, f, neuter), 3 numbers (singular, dual, plural), 6 cases (nom., gen., dat., acc., instr., loc., voc.), in 6 main declensions. Verb distinguished 5 moods (indic., imperative, conditional, infin., supine), 3 simple tenses (pres., aorist, impf.), 1 voice (active), 5 participles (present and 2 past active, present and past passive).

Numerals: [jedinŭ dŭva trije četuire petĭ šestĭ sedmĭ osmĭ devetĭ desetĭ] 100 == [sŭto] (Compare Russian etc., Sanskrit).

Chuvassian (Chuvash)

(AL/tk) 1·4 m (in 1939) on the R. Volga south east of Kazan. DD Upper C. or Viryal; Lower C. or Anatri. A distinctive and somewhat divergent Turkic language, with borrowings from Arabic and Persian as well as Russian and east Fennic languages. Literature, in a modified Cyrillic alphabet, dates from C18 and has been expansive in all fields since the Revolution.

Coptic*

(HS/eg) The direct descendant of ancient Egyptian,

employed by the Christian Copts from C3. Ousted as
spoken vernacular by Arabic from C12, it was spoken by a
few elderly people in C15 and by C19 was reserved almost
entirely as a cultural language—though there are thought
to have been one or two villages where it was still in use. It
remains in use now only as a liturgical language, although
some attempts are being made at its revival. (DD: Bohairic,
the major dialect; Sahidic[x]; Akhimimic[x]; Fayyumic[x];
Memphitic[x]). See also Egyptian[x].

Cornish[x] (Kernwys)

(IE/ct.b) The language of Cornwall (see Celtic—Brythonic), a development (as Welsh) of the language of the
ancient Britons from C5AD, and at that time carried to
Brittany, whence the Breton language. Represented as a
distinct language from C9 texts, a vocabulary from C12,
and religious dramas CC16–17. Last native speaker died
1777, though still learnt by enthusiasts. Numerals: onen
deu try peswar pymp whegh seyth eth naw dek, 100 = kans.
(Compare Welsh).

Corsican ?

Cracovian
D of Polish, qv.

Croatian
see Serbo-Croat.

Curian
D of Latvian, qv.

Cushite LL
(HS/cs.c) Major group of the Cushitic Semitic languages
covering main coastal regions of Ethiopia and Somalia,
consisting of Afar, Agaw, Beja, Galla, Saho, Somali; qqv.

Cushitic LL
(HS/cs) Semitic languages occupying the Horn of Africa

in a delta-shaped area, and consisting of the Cushite proper languages (cs/c, see entry above) and Sidama⁰, qv. A third branch, Meroitic, is extinct. None of these languages has a written literature, and they have been studied only since the end of C19.

Czech (Česky)

(IE/sv.w) 10 m, western Czechoslovakia (Bohemia, Moravia, and part of Silesia). DD: in Bohemia, Central D (the standard, region of Prague), North-eastern D, South-western D, Czecho-Moravian D (transition between Czech and Slovak); in Moravia, the Hanak DD (around Brno and Prostějov); in Silesia, the Lach DD form a transition to Polish and are similar to eastern Slovak. The distinction between Czech and Slovak is largely due to the dominance of the central dialect (in each case) rather than of the form transitional between them.

Until C13, Czech words known only from glosses in Latin texts from the important medieval state of Bohemia. The growth of Czech power resulted in the development of literary Czech, and the founding of Prague University in 1348 ushered in a period of great Czech influence on surrounding countries. Hence Czech provides the earliest great Slavonic literature and is the most distinctive of Slavonic LL. Dialect of Prague established as standard in early C15, with improved orthography and purging of archaisms and Germanisms by John Hus, the religious reformer. Modern standard based on grammar of Gebauer, 1894.

Czech vowel mutation, C14, distinguished it from other Slavonic LL, even from Slovak; dual number, and use of aorist and imperfect have been discarded. Roman alphabet used. Numerals: jedan dva tři čtyři pět šest sedm osm devět deset, 100 = sto (Cf. Church Slavonic, Russian).

D

Dalmatian LL[x]

(IE/rm) Extinct group of Romance languages formerly occupying the Adriatic coast from island of Veglia to Ragusa (Dubrovnik, S. Yugoslavia). Ragusan extinct since beginning C17; Vegliote, last native speaker died 1880.

Dameli

D of Kafir[o], qv.

Danish (Dansk)

(IE/gm.n) 4·8 m, Denmark, including aberrant Jutish dialect. Closely related to Swedish, with which it comprises the eastern branch of Scandinavian languages. Distinct literary language from C13. Official language of Norway during Danish rule CC15–19, with far-reaching effects on Norwegian language, qv. Numerals: en to tre fire fem seks syv otte ni ti, 100 = hundrede. (cf Swedish, Icelandic).

Primitive Scandinavian, from which the modern languages are derived, seems to have spread northwards from a Danish home during C1AD, and the term Danish applies to this as well as to the Scandinavian languages in general up to C13.

Dankali

= Afar, qv.

Dardic[o]

(IE/ia.nw) 1·5 m in N.W. India. A series of related dialects: Shina (town and surroundings of Gilgit, 68 th speakers); Kohistani (3·5 th); Kashmiri, qv.

Dargwa (Dargin)

(CC.N./e) 108 th (in 1926) Caucasian language, elevated to status of literary language since the Revolution, under

Soviet encouragement, and using a basically Cyrillic script with an admixture of Roman and other symbols to incorporate its rich sound system.

Dayak
(MP/in) 1·25 m in interior of Borneo. Several dialects. An Indonesian language related to Malay, qv for description.

Demotic Greek
see Greek (Modern).

Dravidian
(DV) The languages of S. India, spoken by c100 m (25% of population), receding before Indo-Aryan languages but still very vigorous. Unlike other speeches of India, these appear to be indigenous and probably once extended over at least the whole of the country, as suggested by the isolation of Brahui (DV) in Iran. They may be distantly connected with the URALIAN family, but nothing definite has been proved.

All use native alphabets based on Devanagari, and some, such as Tamil and Canarese, boast a rich literary tradition.

Though varied, the languages are demonstrably akin. Word formation by suffixes; nouns distinguished by status (inferior/superior); parts of speech restricted to nouns, pronouns and verbs; verb shows distinction between affirmative and negative voices. For representative numerals, see Tamil.

Dutch (Nederlandsch)
(IE/gm.w) 13 m in Netherlands; variants Flemish and Afrikaans account for further 4 m; Dutch colonial empire includes 60 m, mainly Indonesia and Dutch Guiana.

Origins in Low German DD of Franks and Saxons (cf. English, Frisian), distinct by middle of C12AD, period of Old Dutch to middle C16. Now gaining ground over Flemish in the north of Belgium. Numerals: een tvee drie

vier vijf zes zeven acht negen tien, 100 = honderd. (Cf
German). See also Afrikaans, Flemish.

E

Egyptian
  D of Arabic, qv.

Egyptian[x]
  (HS/eg) The ancient language of Egypt became extinct
about C4AD. Reconstructions and comparison with Coptic*
show it to have been a Hamitic language and related to the
Semitic ancestor of Arabic, although the latter itself is not
recorded before C6AD. The direct descendant of Egyptian
proper is Coptic (qv) which may have lingered on as a
vernacular until C19. Since Coptic is still the liturgical
language of the Coptic Church, Egyptian, in the broad sense,
can claim over four thousand years of history in the same
area, the only rival to this record being Chinese. (Modern
Egyptian, being a dialect of Arabic, is not closely related).

Engadinish
  = Rumansch, see Rheto-Romance LL.

English
  (IE/gm.w) 300 m; United Kingdom, USA, Canada,
Australia, New Zealand, officially second to Afrikaans in
South Africa and to Hindi in India. Most widespread
language of civilization, both culturally and commercially.
  Origins in Saxon DD carried over from N. Germany
C5AD (cf. Dutch and see Saxon). Old English (Anglo-
Saxon) from CC8–11 in three major groups: Anglian
(including Northumbrian and Mercian), West Saxon
(Wessex) and Kentish, corresponding respectively to settle-
ments of Angles, Saxons and Jutes. Linguistic influences
from Scandinavian languages through Viking invasions

during most of this period. Middle English was ushered in by the Norman conquest and politically subordinated to Norman French. By the time English was re-established as the official language of law and administration in late C14 it had undergone profound changes, principally in the simplification of inflections and the incorporation of much Norman French (today about 50% of English vocabulary is of Romance origin, dating largely from this period).

These changes were common to all varieties of English, and the modern language may be said to begin with the coalescence of former dialects into a London standard based mainly on Mercian, from the end of C14.

The spread of English throughout the world has been principally due to exploration and colonization, but its status as an international medium of communication can be ascribed to its intrinsic flexibility and richness. While withstanding the assaults of Scandinavian and French in its early history, it has profited considerably by extensive borrowing from them, and thereby acquired a facility for incorporating foreign elements into its ample phonetic system and straightforward grammatical pattern, resulting in a rich vocabulary with an international flavour.

Dialectal variations of English are slight, and occur mainly in the realm of accent and pronunciation. The pattern of present-day English is guided to a considerable extent by American usage, which has led some writers to refer to 'Anglo-American' rather than 'English'. In fact this is not an inappropriate term, for the content and structure of the language are again undergoing fundamental changes which may eventually necessitate a term to replace 'Modern English', while widespread daily communication between the two countries in politics, commerce, culture and entertainment is sufficiently intensive to suggest that the British and American varieties are more likely to coalesce than to diverge yet further.

Erse

= Scots Gaelic, qv; sometimes incorrectly applied to Irish Gaelic. It derives from *Ersch*, which is the Scots word meaning 'Irish'; since Scots Gaelic is derived from the Irish in any case, the confusion is understandable.

Eskimo[o]

(AMR) A group of dialects constituting the northernmost branch of the Amerindian languages (qv). Owing to its small but distinctive sound system (21 basic sounds) and highly polysynthetic nature, Eskimo has hitherto been written either in an unsatisfactory syllabery provided by 19th century missionaries, or, for linguistic studies, in the phonetic alphabet. Recently the Canadian Department for Northern Affairs commissioned the production of an adapted Roman alphabet, and published in September 1965 a folk-tale in that script. Thus equipped with an official orthography it is likely that the dialect used may become a literary and linguistic standard.

Estonian

(UR/fn.b) 900 th speakers in Estonian SSR + 200 th colonists in USSR, and some speakers in Sweden since 1944. Major DD: Reval (in the north); Dorpat (south); Kodavere (contains features from both). Standard: Reval.

Oldest text: *Lullumaa Prayers*, c1525, but it is thought to have been extant in the same area, with Livonian, from C9AD. Extensive popular poetry. The literary language has been polished and elaborated so as to make it as distinctive as possible from Finnish and free from Finnish influences, as a result of which the language is now more complex than it was a century ago.

Related to Finnish, but not so close as to be mutually intelligible; vocabulary loans from Finnish, Low German, Baltic and Slavonic. Vowel harmony only in Reval dialect.

Numerals: üks kaks kolm neli wiis kuus seitse kaheksa
üheksa kümma, 100 = sada. (cf. Finnish).

Estremenho
D of Portuguese, qv.

Ethiopic LL
(HS/eo) The original Semitic Ethiopian language in its
classical form, Ge'ez, qv, now survives as a literary and
liturgical language, but was replaced in C17 by vernaculars
represented by Amharic, Tigre, Tigriña, Harari, Gafat,
Argobba and Gurage, qqv.

Etruscan[x]
(?) The Etruscan civilization of N. Italy flourished CC7-
4BC and was engaged in a constant struggle with the
Romans, until they conquered and incorporated it into the
Roman State, c200BC. The language, which lasted a little
longer, is represented in hundreds of mainly funerary
inscriptions in an alphabet of 26 characters whose history is
unknown. Some interpretations have been made, sufficient
to show that Etruscan was not an Indo-European language
and bore no relation to any other known tongue alive or
dead, and to render further interpretations tantalizingly
problematical—such as the numerals 1—6: δu zal ci ša
maχ huδ, which have been found on the sides of dice but
with no indication of their correct order. The standard
dialect of modern Italian, Tuscan, which is spoken in an
area corresponding to old Etruria, shows distinctive points
of pronunciation which some have ascribed to an Etruscan
substratum.

Euskara
Basque, qv.

Ewe

43

F

Faeroese (Føroyskt)

(IE/gm.n) 26 th in the Faeroes. These islands are a
Danish protectorate, but the people retain a language descended from Old Norse and still very similar to Icelandic,
though phonetic peculiarities prevent these languages from
being mutually intelligible. (Both are quite distinct from
Danish, see Scandinavian LL). Numerals: ein tveir tríggir
fýra fimm seks sjey átta niggju tíggju, 100 = hundrað.
(Cf. Icelandic, Danish).

Farsi

= Persian, qv.

Fennic (Finnic, Somian) LL

A major branch of the URALIAN languages, characterized
by a complex case system and agglutinative structure.
UR/fn.b: Baltic Fennic (Finnish, Estonian, etc)
UR/fn.v: Volgan Fennic (Mordvinian, Cheremissian)
UR/fn.p: Permian (Zyryan, Votiak).

Fijian

(MP/pl) Spoken in Fiji islands by natives of Melanesian
type, though the language appears to be Polynesian.

Finnic

= Fennic, qv.

Finnish (Suomi)

(UR/fn.b) 3—4 m in Finland except in 1) Utsjoki, where
Lappish predominates; and 2) Swedish speaking areas,
namely, the Åland islands and archipelago to the east of
them, and the coastal region of Nyland, south Ostrobotnia.
Also 130 th in USSR, 7 th in Finmark, 250 th speakers in
USA and 2 th in Australia. DD: Suomi (the standard);

*how about Tornedalen in Swede
large Finnish population there.*

Karelian and Olonecian, sometimes classed as separate languages but mutually intelligible with Suomi (see entry under Karelian); Ingermlandian, spoken in a few villages of Ingermland by Greek Catholics whose ancestors emigrated from S.W. Karelia perhaps as early as C12; Ingrian, several hundred speakers in the neighbourhood of Leningrad, surrounded by Karelian but closer to Suomi.

The literary cultivation of Finnish dates from about 1530, and there is a translation of the New Testament of 1548. Until C18 Finland was under the Swedish Constitution, after which the Russians dominated. Under the latter Finnish flourished as a literary medium, though it and Swedish were both official languages until well into C20. Swedish is widely understood, but Finnish is the vernacular of 90% of the population.

Agglutinative structure; nouns distinguish singular/plural but not gender, 16 'cases' by suffixation, but some of these are dropping out in favour of prepositional constructions, verb shows perfect, imperfect, and combined present/future, and a profusion of infinitives and participles. Numerals: yksi kaksi kolme neljä viisi kuusi seitsemän kahdeksan yhdeksän kymmenen; 100 = sata (probably from Indo-European, cf Sanskrit). (Compare Estonian).

Flemish (Vlaamsch)

(IE/gm.w) 5·2 m, Belgium, principally from Brussels northwards, though some as far south as the French side of the border. The rest of the population speaks French.

Basically a Frankish dialect, closely related to Dutch. After lying dormant for 300 years, it was revived by writers in the universally nationalistic nineteenth century, drawing both on the old Flemish dialect and literary Dutch. The spelling is more archaic, and three genders are retained (Dutch has two, and its derivative Afrikaans has coalesced even these). Flemish speakers in general cling tenaciously to their language to preserve it from the encroachment of French from the south and Dutch from the north. The latter is gaining ground, but the University of Ghent remains a stronghold of distinctively Flemish learning and culture.

Franco-Provencal[o]

(IE/rm.g) A group of six dialects spoken in the region of Burgundy and forming a transition between French and Provençal. Despite some C12 literature and its occasional employment by poets as late as C16, it has never crystallized into a spoken standard or distinct literary medium.

French (Français)

(IE/rm.g) 85 m, of whom 47 m in France. Has official status in Belgium, Switzerland, Canada (Quebec), French Guiana and widespread French possessions; also widely current in much of Africa and Indo-China. World–wide prominence as a medium of diplomacy and politics for many years, and universally recognized as a major literary and cultural medium.

Origins: variety of Romance (from Vulgar Latin) current in northern part of Gaul under Roman occupation. Gallo-Romance developed into 2 distinct dialect groups, characterized by word for *yes*—in the north *oïl*, in the south *oc* (hence *Languedoil* and *Languedoc*). Standard French derives from Francien, the *oïl* dialect of the Ile-de-France which achieved prominence through the favoured geographical and political position of Paris. The distinctive character of French, marking it off from Provençal, Spanish, Italian, etc, is due to Germanic influences from Frankish invaders (CC4–5, resulting in change of original language name *Romanz*) and Viking settlers in Normandy, C10. A Gaulish Celtic substratum is also discernible. Earliest record: *Serments de Strasbourg*, 842 AD. Old French CC10–14, Middle French CC15–16. The *Oc* dialects produced Provençal, an important literary language of the Middle Ages but relegated to minor status by French from CC12–13.

The language was more or less fixed by the Académie Française from C17, an institution whose fundamental interest has always been the purity of the French language. It is largely due to this linguistic self-consciousness that minor languages (e.g. Provençal, Catalan, Breton) are not encouraged, and other dialects of French proper (theoretically numbering over a dozen) remain socially unacceptable. Nevertheless there have been numerous borrowings of vocabulary from English, which are not fully in accord with the spirit of the language. Considerable influences of Classical and Italian languages especially during the Renaissance. Numerals: un deux trois quatre cinq six sept huit neuf dix, cent. (Cf Latin, Spanish, Italian).

Frisian (Friesisch)

(IE/gm.w) 300 th speakers in over twenty islands off coasts of northern Holland and western Denmark. Divisible into Eastern, Northern and Western dialect groups.

Descended, like Dutch and English, from old Saxon dialects of northern Germany. Very close to, and mutually intelligible with, English until what are traditionally held as 'recent times', though probably not later than C15 if that. However, Frisian is certainly the closest relation of English; the two are sometimes collectively referred to as Ingweonic, in opposition to the Dutch branch of Low Germanic. Distinctive literary language from C14, at one time more widespread and rival to Dutch in the Netherlands. Numerals: än tâw tri fjâwer fiw säks söwen acht njugen tjin, hunnert. Compare Old English: ān twēgen þrīe fēower fīf siex seofon eahta nigon tīen, hundred.

Friulan

see Rheto-Romance LL.

Fulani

G

Gaelic LL

(IE/ct.g) The Goidelic group (see Celtic—Goidelic) consists of Irish (sometimes incorrectly termed Erse), Scots Gaelic (or Erse), and Manx[x]. These three tongues call themselves 'Gaelic', and are derived from a parent or Common Gaelic current in Ireland during the first few centuries AD. Carried across from there to Scotland and to Man, in C5, Common Gaelic survived as a somewhat archaic literary medium over the whole Gaelic speaking area until as late as C17 in Ireland and C18 in Scotland (Classical Gaelic). The Irish, Scots and Manx vernaculars began to diverge from one another and from Classical Common Gaelic from about C13.

Galician[o] (Galego)

(IE/rm.h) Language or dialect group of Galicia, N.W. Spain, population over 2 m but considerably fewer speakers. Both modern Galician and modern Portuguese derive from a Hispanic dialect current in N.W. Spain in the Middle Ages: the first record of Old Galician dates from 1192, and it became the medium of a rich lyric poetry during CC13–14. It crystallized into Portuguese, pronounced a standard language and encouraged to be as distinct as possible from Spanish during C16. The remnants of Galician drifted into the Castilian Spanish speaking orbit, heavily influenced and relegated to minor standard by Spanish and thus mistakenly regarded as a true dialect thereof.

Galla (Oromi)

(HS/cs.c) 3 m in central Kenya. A Semitic tribal vernacular, with considerable dialectal variation and no written literature. Numerals: [tokko lamma sadi afur šan ǰaa torba saddet sagal kuda] 100 = [dibba].

Garwi

D of Dardic[o], qv.

Gaulish[x]

see Celtic.

Gawarbati

D of Kafir[o], qv.

Ge'ez[x]

(HS/eo) Language of Semitic conquerors in Ethiopia CC3–8AD, derived from a form of South Arabic (qv under that name, as it is distinct from Arabic proper). No records of it during CC9–13, after which time it has been replaced as a spoken tongue by various Ethiopic (qv) vernaculars probably descended from it during this period. It survived as a literary medium, the classical period of its literature being CC13–17. Its principal descendant is Amharic, qv.

Georgian (Kartvelian)

(CC.S) 2·4 m (in 1959), official language of Georgian SSR in Caucasus, the only recognized medium of instruction in University of Tiflis and thus the language of significant publications, especially scientific, emanating from that centre. DD: Imerian, Gurian, Pshav, Thush, Khevzur, Ingilo, Mthiul, Rachin, Kakhetin, Meskh.

Literature from C5AD (translation of Bible). A highly developed cultural and literary language, especially since C19, having profited by influences of surrounding languages such as Russian and Turkish. Numerals: [ert[h]i ori sami ot[h]xi χut[h]i ek[h]vsi švidi rva t[sh]xra at[h]i] 100 = [asi].

German (Deutsch)

(IE/gm.w) 95 m, official status in West and East Germany, Austria, Switzerland; speakers also in Poland, Hungary, Rumania, USSR, North and South America; current in former colonized territories of Africa and the Pacific.

In its broadest sense, German covers all the Germanic dialects of Germany itself, and consists of the Low German DD in the North, Upper German DD in the South, including Austria and Switzerland, and Middle German DD between. In its narrowest sense, German = High German, the standard deriving largely from the Upper Saxon dialect of Meissen (within the Middle DD area) and including some features proceeding originally from the South (especially Austria). High German DD: (Upper German) Austrian, Alemannic, Swabian, Bavarian, East Franconian; (Middle German) Silesian, Upper Saxon, Franconian DD except East Franconian and Low Franconian. Low German, in its broadest sense, includes Flemish, Dutch, Frisian and English as well as Low German in its narrowest sense, i.e. Plattdeutsch, qv. See also Yiddish.

High German DD distinct from those of Low German by C6AD, known in writing from C8AD (The *Hildebrandslied*). No cultural or political centre amongst the many German medieval states, so no dialect predominated, until period of Middle High German (1050—1250). During latter part of this time, the poetic language of the *Minnesänger*, of court Romances and heroic epics, shows conscious avoidance of regionalisms but a marked predominance of southern features (Upper German). From C14, with the beginnings of New High German, dialects of Central German achieved greater prominence. Factors leading to emergence of High German Standard: (1) imperial and territorial chanceries preferred German to Latin for edicts, and for ease of intercommunication avoided regionalisms; (2) improvement of communications leading to wider commercial activities and more contact between dialect speakers; (3) invention of printing. A fourth factor both established the final standard dialect and introduced German as an important cultural medium on the European scene—namely, the rise of Protestantism with Martin Luther, and particularly his translation of the Bible (1534) into the (East Middle German) dialect of Upper Saxony. The final ratification of the status of Upper Saxon may be for convenience dated 1748, with the appearance of Gottsched's *Deutsche Sprachkunst*. Significant as a literary medium especially from C18; as a philosophical and scientific medium from C19. Modern German dialects remain distinctive, and educated speakers may be broadly placed by their pronunciation though not actually speaking or even knowing their regional dialect. There is a standard pronunciation for the stage (*Deutsche Bühnenaussprache*).

German has had little influence on major European languages (except Hungarian); conversely it is very self-sufficient, preferring to draw on native vocabulary for new expressions where others (English, French etc) draw on Latin and Greek; e.g. *television* = *Fernsehen*, where *Fern* = *tele-* = '*far*', & *sehen* = *vision* = '*seeing*'; *hydrogen* = *Wasserstoff*, where *Wasser* = *hydro-* = '*water*', & *-stoff* = *-gen-* = '*substance*'. High German differs from the Low German languages (English, Dutch etc) in retaining a highly synthetic (inflected) structure. Noun has three genders, four cases and a variety of plural formations; adjective agrees when used epithetically and follows either a strong or a weak declension; verb has infinitive, two participles, subjunctive, and a true present and preterite—other tenses are composed. Numerals: eins zwei drei vier fünf sechs sieben acht neun zehn, 100 = hundert (cf Dutch, Danish).

He's nuts.

Germanic LL

(IE/gm) Branch of INDO-EUROPEAN including German, English, Dutch and Scandinavian languages. Proto-Germanic formed with Celtic and Italic a fairly distinctive western European group, but bore some similarities to Baltic and Slavonic. Primitive Germanic split, probably by C1AD, into three branches; the Western branch split,

probably by 6CAD into High and Low divisions; Scandinavian languages distinctive, but not distinct from one
another until cC15AD.

gm.e (Eastern group) Gothic[x] and other extinct languages or dialects (Burgundian, Vandalic, Skirian,
Rugian).

gm. n (Northern or Scandinavian): East Scand.—
Danish, Swedish (inc. Gutnic), Norwegian Riksmål;
West Scand.—Norwegian Landsmål, Icelandic, Faeroese;

gm.w (Western) High German LL—German, Lango-
bardic[x]; Low German LL—(Saxon type) English,
Frisian, Plattdeutsch; (Franconian type) Flemish, Dutch,
Afrikaans (from Dutch).

Geg (Gheg)
D of Albanian, qv.

Ghilaki
D of Mazandarani, qv.

Gilyak (Nivkh)
(PS/gl) 4 th (in 1926), a Palaeo-Siberian language of
North Sakhalin and around mouth of Amur river. Used in
schools and as cultural language under Soviet encouragement since 1929.

Gitan
= Romany, qv.

Goidelic LL
see Gaelic.

Gold
see Tungusic.

Gondi
(DV) 2 m speakers scattered over Gondwana region, now
giving way to Hindi.

Gothic[x]

(IE/gm.e) Thought to be the language of Scandinavia before advent of the 'Danish Tongue', as suggested by the name of the Swedish region of Gotland, as well as by peculiarities of Gutnic dialect of Swedish, which may be due to Gothic substratum. Goths spread towards Black Sea and founded a kingdom, about C3AD. Carried across Europe by Ostrogoths and Visigoths; overcome by Romance in Spain, C8; some Gothic speakers reported in Crimea as late as C16. Known principally from Wulfila's translation of the Bible, C4AD. Numerals: ains twái þrija fidwor fims saíhs sibun ahtáu niun taíhun, 100 = taíhunte-hund. (Compare German).

Grabar

= Armenian, qv.

Greek (Ancient or Classical)

(IE/gk). Language of the Hellenes who spread in waves southwards into Greece in C13BC. Known to exist in the middle of the second millennium BC; earliest inscriptions from Abu Simbel, on the Nile, 591BC. Greek alphabet derived from Phoenician. DD Aeolic, Ionic, Attic, Achaean (Arcadian and Cyprian), Doric, Lesbian, Laconian, Cretan. All of these probably mutually intelligible. By C4BC Attic, the Classical Greek based on the dialect of Athens, predominated as a literary medium, forming a standard language or Koiné, from which modern Greek is descended. The Greek of the New Testament is the spoken Koiné of C1AD. Other dialects died or were incorporated (with two possible exceptions, see next entry).

Greek (Modern)

(IE/gk) 11 m speakers, of whom 8·5 m in Greece; others in European Turkey, USSR, Bulgaria, South America.

Developed from the Classical standard (Koiné, see

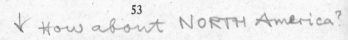
How about NORTH America?

previous entry), Modern Greek may be said to start with the language of the New Testament. It has given rise to further dialectal variants, but not to any great extent; in fact Greek has changed very little in three thousand years. Two dialects seem aberrant: Tsakonian, east coast of the Peloponnese, has archaic features which suggest direct descent from the Laconian[x] dialect (see previous entry), which was spoken in the same region; and Maniote, found in southern Italy, may date from the Greek colonisation of Italy CC8–BC.

The modern Greek standard, termed *Katheravousa*, predominantly a literary medium, is at present being encouraged by the Church and state education in preference to the somewhat divergent vernacular, termed *Romaic* or *Demotic* Greek. Katheravousa is considerably closer in morphology and syntax to the classical Koiné.

Noun has three genders, three cases; adjective agrees; verb has active and passive conjugations, true present, past (definite) and imperfect, and composes other tenses. Numerals: *ēnas dúo treîs tēssereis pēnte êxi eptā oktō enniā dēka*, 100 = *ekatō*. (Compare Latin, Sanskrit).

Guancha[x]

(HS/bb) Extinct dialect of the Canary Islands; some inscriptions, and elements of vocabulary attested by various authors from C14. Gave way to Spanish, C16. Probably a dialect of Berber[o], qv.

Gujerati

(IE/ia.w) 16 m in the Gujarat region of W. India. A literary medium since C15.

Gurage[o]

(HS/eo) 350 th speakers of a group of Ethiopic dialects, south west of Addis-Ababa. DD: Chaha, Muher, Aymallal, Eza, Walani, and others. No literature; and giving way to Amharic.

Gurani⁰

(IE/ir.w) A dialect group in western Iran, closely related to Zaza⁰ and more distinctly to Persian; considerably influenced by the contiguous Kurdish⁰ dialects. Records from C18.

Gutnish (Gutnic)

D of Swedish, qv.

Gypsy

= Romany, qv.

H

Hainanese

D of Chinese, qv.

Hakka

D of Chinese, qv.

Hamito-Semitic

(HS) An important family among whose members are reckoned Arabic, Hebrew, Ethiopic and Berber languages, and ancient Egyptian, and occupying the greater part of northern Africa and the Near East.

These languages are characterized by word construction based on consonantal roots, i.e. a sequence of two or three consonants denotes a general idea—in itself not necessarily substantival or verbal—whose exact grammatical function in the context is defined by an intervening sequence of vowels.

Relationships have been sought between HAMITO-SEMITIC and other families, principally INDO-EUROPEAN and CAUCAS-AN, but with little success.

(1) The Semitic languages form a coherent group, and as such are dealt with under that heading, where can also be

found examples of consonantal roots. Their connection with the more heterogeneous Hamitic languages has been long suspected but only recently established. A period of Common or Proto-Hamito-Semitic must date back to the fifth millennium BC.

(2) 'Hamitic' is a loose term denoting neither a true ethnic nor a precise linguistic group. The various languages are for the most part spoken by nomads, lacking a written literature and almost everywhere subordinated to Semitic languages such as Arabic and Amharic. Since the extinction of ancient Egyptian (C4BC), none has achieved eminence as a language of state, culture or commerce. The relationship of Hamitic to certain groups of Negro African languages is being investigated: some obvious Hamitic or Hamitic-derived features of Hausa and its close neighbours have led some to propose a further branch of Hamitic ('Chad') to include them.

Semitic:
HS/nw: North west group (Hebrew, Aramaic etc.)
/ab: Arabic
/sa: South Arabic
/eo: Ethiopic (Amharic, etc)
Hamitic:
/eg: Egyptian[x], Coptic*.
/cs: Cushitic (cs.c = Cushite LL, cs.s = Sidama[o])
/bb: Berber languages and dialects.

Harari

(HS/eo) 35 th in and around town of Harar, Ethiopia. The speakers are mainly Muslim, resulting in considerable Arabic influence, but the language is giving way to Amharic. Literature includes some songs; not recorded before C16.

Hausa

?(NAF.) or (HS/Chad) 13 m speakers in the Central

Sudan and northern part of Nigeria, only 4 m of whom are actually Hausa people. Like Swahili in the southern part of the continent, Hausa has become an important and wide-spread language of commerce and general communications. See also NEGRO-AFRICAN. Numerals: [ʔdaja biju uku huʔdu bijar šidda bakwai takwas tara goma].

Hawaian (Hawai'ian)

(MP/pl) 70 th or fewer. Related to Samoan, Tongan, Maori (see MALAYO-POLYNESIAN), but now receding fast before American English.

Hazara

D of Mongolian, qv.

Hebrew

(HS/nw) 1 m, Israel, and living language of culture and liturgy in Jewish communities throughout the world.

Inscriptions from C9BC, Old Testament CC9–7BC but *Song of Deborah* (Judges, V) may be earlier than 1,000 BC. Thus Hebrew has a history of over three thousand years, vying in age only with Chinese and Coptic.

Originally the widespread speech of the ancient Canaan ow region, its decline began with the capture of Jerusalem and removal of Jews to Babylon: by C3–2BC it had been largely replaced by Aramaic as a vernacular. Carried over the world by the wandering Jews as the literary and litur-gical language of Judaism it has continued to serve as a cultural medium of international communication amongst Jews whose everyday speech would be German, French, Spanish, etc. In countries where extensive Jewish settlement took place during the Middle Ages, hybrid languages grew up as the result of hebraızıng the surrounding tongues—hence Yiddish (qv) from German, and Ladino from Spanish.

A movement to re-establish Hebrew as the everyday

vernacular of the Jews in Israel began at the end of C19
and has been remarkably successful. It has been the official
language of administration, the press, and education in
Israel since 1919. Little difficulty has been found in adapting
it to modern linguistic needs, for the rich literature of
Hebrew provides a stockpile of roots for new vocabulary (in
the same way as English draws on Latin and Greek, Hindi
on Sanskrit, and modern on ancient Chinese), and borrowings are made from European languages through Yiddish
and Ladino. Arabic is also a major source, as it is Hebrew's
closest spoken relative and was formerly the language of
the majority of the inhabitants in the region where Hebrew
is now official.

For general description, see Semitic. Numerals (absolute
form, following noun and in apposition to it): [ʔeχād
šnajim šlošāh ʔarbāçāh χamĭšāh šiššāh šivçāh šmōnāh
tišçāh çasārāh] 100 = [mēʔāh]. (Compare Arabaic).

Hellenic
= Greek, qv.

Hindi (Hindustani, Urdu)

(IE/ia.c) 175 m, the official language of India. Since the
name 'Hindi' can refer to about half a dozen linguistic items,
the terminology is somewhat confusing, and should be
clarified, as follows:

(1) *Hindi* is a broad name covering two contiguous groups
of dialects in the central part of northern India; these are
referred to as East Hindi and West Hindi, whose entries
follow this section.

(2) *Hindustani* is the principal dialect of the *West Hindi*
group, and has become the *lingua franca* of India since its
use in the cosmopolitan bazaar attached to the old Delhi
Court and its spread by officials of the Mogul Empire.
Hindustani is the standard spoken vernacular of India; it
appears also however in two literary forms:

(3) *Urdu*, written in Arabic script and drawing on Arabic and Persian vocabulary, and

(4) *Literary Hindi*, representing a reaction against the foreign nature of Urdu, written in native Devanagari script and drawing, where necessary, on its ancestor Sanskrit for new vocabulary.

As the result of its widespread use among people of varying linguistic traditions (Dravidian, Munda, etc), Hindustani has become much simplified in structure: considerable reduction of gender and case system in nouns; adjectives indeclinable; one basic verbal paradigm. Numerals: [ek do tīn čār pāŋč čha sāt āth nau das] 100 = [sau, sai]. (Compare Sanskrit, Persian).

Hindi, Eastern DD

(IE/ia.c) 7 m speakers from Cawnpore to the Benares. Principal dialects: Awadhi, Bagheli, Chhattisgarhi.

Hindi, Western DD

(IE/ia.c) 71 m, including 65 m native speakers of principal dialect Hindustani, between Cawnpore and the Punjabi frontier. Other dialects include Braj (which has literary status), Kanauji, Bundeli, Bangaru.

Hittite[x]

(IE) Language of the Hittite Empire which flourished in Asia Minor CC19–14BC, and was overcome by the Phrygian invasion of 1200BC. It is known from tablets found at Boghazkoy in 1905, written in an Akkadian cuneiform syllabery, of political, religious and legal content. Since their decipherment in 1916–17 it has been established that Hittite was an Indo-European language—thus related to the ancestors of Germanic, Italic, Slavonic, etc—but represented a considerably earlier offshoot than any other known branch, thus pushing back into even remoter antiquity the period during which the hypothetical Indo-European parent language may have been spoken.

Ho

  D of Bhili⁰, qv.

Hottentot

  see KHOIN.

Hungarian (Magyar)

  (UR/ug) 14 m, Hungary, speakers also in Slovakia,
Yugoslavia, Rumania. The major non-Indo-European
language of Europe, it is widely separated from its Uralian
relatives (Estonian, Finnish, Samoyedic etc in the extreme
north of Europe and western Asia), and has the further
distinctions of being the oldest known Uralian language,
and having the greatest number of speakers amongst them.
The language is furthermore extremely homogeneous, eight
theoretical dialects being practically indistinguishable.

  Origins: brought into southern Europe by the Magyars,
who conquered Moldavia (now Hungary) in C9. Earliest
record: funeral oration C13, and a hymn of the same period.
Hungarian has been influenced by the currency of Latin as
a cultural and literary language until C19, and by the
proximity of German for a thousand years. Also noticeable
are a Slavonic influence and a number of loan-words from
Ossete. A reaction against German at the end of C18 led to
a rich and flourishing Hungarian literature.

  A remarkably full and complex language. Its rich
phonetic system, including elaborate consonant clusters,
requires the Roman alphabet extended to 44 characters by
means of digraphs and diacritic marks. Prominent vowel
harmony; front, neutral and back distinguished. Two
numbers, no gender, six declensions, officially four cases,
by suffixation, but agglutinative structure leads to suffixed
postpositions giving the impression of more cases. Adjective
mainly invariable. Rich verbal system: conjugations for
definite and indefinite, according to whether subject speci-
fically mentioned, three moods of four tenses each, five

aspects, four participles; and the infinitive can be person-alized. Numerals: egy kettő három négy őt hat hét nyolc kilenc tíz; 100 = száz.

Hyperborean
= PALAEOSIBERIAN, qv.

I

Iberian

It is generally thought that Basque (qv) is the last des-cendant of an Iberian group of languages formerly wide-spread over the Iberian peninsular. Short Iberian inscriptions have been preserved, the longest being that of the Alcoy lead-tablet. Though antedating modern Basque by over 1000 years the language reveals many points of similarity.

Icelandic (Íslenzka)

(IE/gm.n) 190 th, Iceland. Belonging with Faeroese and Norwegian (Landsmål) to the western group of Scandi-navian, qv, as distinct from Danish and Swedish.

The language has remained practically unchanged, apart from some phonetic developments, since the time of the great Norse sagas (CC10–12) which were written largely in the Icelandic dialect of Old Norse. Its purity is due to several factors: (1) lack of linguistic substratum, since Iceland was unoccupied until the Norse settlements of 874AD onwards; (2) no invasions by foreign speakers, though under Danish rule for centuries until independence in 1945; so far little affected by English from American bases since World War II; (3) isolation. Thus the language is extremely homogeneous, there being practically no dialectal or social variations of speech.

Literary tradition dating from the medieval sagas has remained remarkably virile, to the extent that literature is still said to be the national pastime of all classes. Roman alphabet includes symbols þ and ð, current in all Germanic languages during the Middle Ages but retained only by Icelandic, denoting respectively unvoiced and voiced English *th* (þ as in *thick*, ð as in *this*. Faeroese retains ð but not þ.)

By comparison with other Scandinavian languages its grammar remains archaic and complex. Three genders, four cases. Numerals: einn tveir þrir fjórir fimm sex sjö átta níu tíu, hundrað. (Compare Danish).

Illyrian[x]

(IE/il) As a language it is known from a three word inscription in Greek alphabet found near Scutari, was presumably current in Albania before the time of Christ, and in contact with Germanic, Greek and Italic. Its position suggests that it may have been the ancestor of modern Albanian, qv, which is certainly distinct from other Indo-European languages, but there is nothing concrete to suggest that the two are even related. A further hypothesis attaches to it in an 'Illyrian' group the extinct Venetic, Messapian and Philistine languages.

Indo-Aryan LL

(IE/ia) A branch of INDO-EUROPEAN represented historically by Sanskrit*, qv, and recently by its linguistic descendants in north and west India, principally Hindi. The nearest related group is Iranian, chief representative Persian; the two are sometimes collectively termed Indo-Iranian.

The Indo-Aryan languages and dialects number over 300, few of them with true language status but broadly divisible into groups (see below). They are spoken by about 300 m people. (Other Indian languages include the Dravidian and Munda groups, not related).

Major languages and dialect groups:

ia/nw: North-west (Kafir, Kalasha, Pashai, Tihari, Khowar, Dardic)

/w: West (Lahnda, Sindhi, Gujerati, Marathi, Bhili, Khandesi Rajasthani)
/c: Central (Punjabi, Pahiri, Nepali, Hindi)
/e: East (Bengali, Bihari, Oriya, Assamese)
/s: Singhalese
/r: Romany (Gypsy)
See also Sanskrit*, Pali*.

Indo-Chinese
= SINITIC, qv.

Indo-European
(IE) The Indo-European family of languages covers most of Europe as well as Iran and northern India (hence its name, though the term INDO-GERMANIC is still used mainly by German philologists; the alternative ARYAN has been dropped, partly owing to its imprecision), and has produced more major languages of civilization than any other family, including as it does Latin, Greek, Sanskrit, English, French, Spanish and Russian.

It was the discovery in C18 of the old classical language of India, Sanskrit, which led to the concept of linguistic evolution and language relationships, for Sanskrit bears affinities with Latin and Greek which suggested the possibility of a common origin for all three. Further relations were seen in Celtic, Germanic, etc, and the study of Indo-European relationships had become far advanced by the end of C19, setting the pattern for investigations into other language groups.

An Indo-European family presupposes the existence at some time in remote antiquity of a unified, primitive Indo-European parent language, whose dialects developed into the ancestors of the present major groups (see below). Such a language cannot be described in detail nor assigned to a satisfactorily datable period, nor can the race or where-

INDO-EUROPEAN

abouts of its speakers be demonstrably stated. It is probable, however, that the home of Indo-European lay in Europe somewhere between the Baltic and the Black Sea, and that it was already differentiated into dialects before waves of migrants carried it westwards to the Atlantic and eastwards into Asia.

It may have been contiguous with URALIAN, but at a time too remote to give any basis for relating the two families. Present day languages of Europe NOT belonging to this family include Basque, Hungarian (and its Uralian relatives such as Finnish and Estonian) and the Caucasian languages.

Extinct branches to which reference may be found in this dictionary: Hittite, Tocharian, Illyrian.

Features common to Indo-European languages include clear formal distinction of noun and verb, a basically inflective structure, and decimal numeration. Comparison of the numerals of known IE languages suggest the following roots—their extremely hypothetical nature is indicated by the preceding asterisks. 1 *oi-, sem-, 2 *du-, 3 *tri, 4 *k^wet, 5 *pénk^we, 6 *seks, 7 *septm̥, 8 *oktō, 9 *new- , 10 *dékm̥, 100 *km̥tóm. These may be compared with those of any IE language given in this dictionary.

IE/gm: Germanic (English, Dutch, German, etc)
/rm: Romance (derived from Latin: French, Spanish, Italian etc)
/it: Italic (Latin and extinct related tongues of Italy)
/ct: Celtic (Gaelic, Welsh, Breton, etc)
/gk: Greek
/al: Albanian
/ar: Armenian
/bt: Baltic (Lithuanian, Latvian)
/sv: Slavonic (Russian, Polish, Serbo-Croat, etc)
/ir: Iranian (Persian, Kurdish, Ossete, etc)
/ia: Indo-Aryan (derived from Sanskrit: Hindi, Bengali etc)

Close relationships exist between Italo-Romance and Celtic, and between these and Germanic, forming a fairly distinct western group. Greek, Albanian and Armenian are each comparatively isolated, sharing many features however with the eastern branches, though Greek shows points of comparison with the western. Many of the comparatively close similarities between Baltic and Slavonic may be due to parallel but independent developments; they are often grouped together as Balto-Slavonic. Iranian and Indo-Aryan are more closely connected, and share some features with Baltic and Slavonic which unite them loosely in an eastern IE group.

Indonesian

(1) for Indonesian LL, see MALAYO-POLYNESIAN.

(2) official language of the Indonesian Republic, called 'Indonesian' but basically Malay, qv.

Ingweonic LL

(IE/gm.w) Term uniting English and Frisian as distinct from other Low Germanic languages (Dutch and its derivatives).

Interamnese

D of Portuguese, qv.

Iranian LL

(IE/ir) A branch of INDO-EUROPEAN consisting of a series of heterogeneous languages and dialect groups mainly in Iran, represented chiefly by Persian.

IE/ir.e: East (Pushto or Afghan, Pamirian°, etc)

/ir.w: West (Persian, Kurdish°, Mazandarani, Baluchi etc)

/ir.o: Ossete, an isolated and aberrant Iranian language of the Caucasus.

Irish (Gaelic)

(IE/ct.g) Approx. 10th, Eire. DD Southern (Munster), Western (Connaught), Northern (Donegal). Official language of the Irish Republic, though most speakers bilingual with, if not monoglot in, English. See also Gaelic LL.

Short inscriptions in Ogam (alphabet) C5AD relate to Gaelic before its differentiation into Irish, Scots and Manx varieties. Short religious texts CC8–10, in Roman script and its Irish derivative, Erse. From C11 Irish flourished in one of the greatest literatures of the Middle Ages, but by C19 had largely given way to English. Present attempts to produce an entirely Irish-speaking population in the Republic are not proving very successful, despite the compulsory teaching of it in state education. This may be partly due to its complex, archaic and impractical orthography: (although officially simplified in the early 1950's): it may be noted that Welsh, with its practically phonetic spelling, is holding its own despite less favourable political circumstances. But again, where emigrated Welsh-speakers tend to keep their language (as for example in Patagonia), Irish emigrants tend to lose theirs. Numerals: aon dô trí ceathair cûig sé seacht ocht naoi deich, 100 = céad. (Compare Welsh, Latin).

Ishkashimi

D of Pamirian°, qv.

Italian (Italiano)

(IE/rm.i) 65 m, official in Italy and Switzerland (50 m and 300 th respectively), current in Lybia and Eritrea, cultural second language eastern Adriatic coast, Tunisia, Egypt, Ethiopia, widely retained by immigrants of N and S America. Numerous DD, Standard is Tuscan.

Origins: geographically the most direct descendant of Latin. While Ecclesiastical Latin remained the language of learning and liturgy during the Middle Ages, the spoken or

Vulgar Latin of the populace was diverging considerably, and rendering the ecclesiastical variety unintelligible to it. In addition, it produced a variety of dialects differing markedly amongst themselves, since Italy is a mountainous country and its dialectal regions were formerly isolated. Earliest records: between CC8–10 glosses in vernacular-Latin-cum-early-Italian were inserted in legal documents for the benefit of those who could not understand Latin proper, indicating the distinction of Italian by that time. Late C11 produces a stereotyped form of Penitential and Absolution, and late C12 a poetic fragment.

Italian literature came into its own in lyrical compositions from the court society of Sicily early C13 under the influence of Provençal lyric poetry. Later the Tuscan dialect was to predominate, in the writings of Dante, Petrarch and Boccaccio. In 1303 Dante wrote a thesis *De Vulgari Eloquantia*, in which he enumerated 14 Italian dialects and failed to find the source of literary Italian—dismissing Latin proper from this post as artificial and incomprehensible to the populace. Although the standard is now the *lingua toscana* based on the educated speech of Florence, the other Italian dialects have continued to flourish and remain socially acceptable (unlike French dialects in France).

Like other Romance languages, Italian has become more analytic in structure. Genders reduced to two, with simpler plural forms, and formal case system lost. Numerals: uno due tre quattro cinque sei sette otto nove dieci, cento. (Compare Latin, French).

Italic LL

(IE/it) The term Italic is generally taken to include the Romance languages, (i.e. those descended from Latin), Latin itself, and certain extinct languages of Italy known to have been closely related to Latin.

In this dictionary a division of labour has been effected, thus:

(1) *Romance* languages (IE/rm): those derived from Latin (Italian, French, etc; see appropriate entry);

(3) *Italic*[x] languages: Latin itself, the old language of Latium; and its close relatives—Faliscan, Umbrian, Oscan, all of which were current in C4BC.

(3) Where necessary, the term *Italo-Romance* is used to refer to these groups, as a distinct branch of INDO-EUROPEAN.

In addition, two further terms may be encountered in general philological reading:

(4) *Italo-Celtic* refers to a period of inferred unity of these Indo-European branches, since they share some close features distinguishing them from Germanic, the third member of the western IE group.

(5) *Pre-Italic* refers to the native languages of Italy prior to the arrival of Indo-European dialects.

See: Latin★, Romance LL.

Iverian

see CAUCASIAN languages.

J

Japanese (Nihongo)
(JP) 100 m, Japan. Also, mainly owing to expansive activities of early this century, speakers in Formosa, Sakhalin, parts of China, Hawaii, Caroline and Marshall islands. DD: some very distinctive since cultural regions have maintained their individuality over many centuries; from north to south: Tohuku, Hoko-Riku, Kanto (inc. Tokyo & Yokohama), Tokkaido, Kinki, Izumo, Shugoku, Sikoku, Kyusu (inc. Satsuma and the distinctive D of Nagasaki), and the DD of Ryu-kyu island region which remained independent from the Japanese Empire until 1872 and so evolved

separately. Not related to Chinese. Possibly connected with Korean, and with it might form a far eastern group of the Altaic LL (Turkish, Mongolian etc).

Early records: Inscriptions from C5AD in Chinese characters, some of them employed for their phonetic value, which is a Japanese feature. A semi-historical treatise dates from 712. Embryonic state of Yamato established CC7–8, language of court standardized in written form called *Bungo*, C10. Subsequently replaced by *Hyozungo*, a compromise between written and spoken varieties. This is the basis of the modern standard, *Kokogo* (National Language) or *Nihongo* (Japanese). Great influence of Chinese from earliest times.

Script: early Japanese, having no script, made use of Chinese ideographic characters. Each ideograph stands for a semantic or grammatical concept, represented in spoken Chinese by a single indeclinable word. Japanese however is agglutinative in structure and therefore requires flexional suffixes. Thus certain ideographs were simplified and used for their purely phonetic or syllabic value. These symbols, termed *Kana*, provide in themselves a fairly satisfactory syllabery without the addition of the original ideographs. They appear in two forms, *Hiragana*, and the more formal *Katakana*. Japanese can be more satisfactorily written in Roman alphabet, and attempts have been made from the end of C19 to introduce and standardize this method. Tradition is very strong, however, and comparatively little headway has been made.

Japanese literature has been rich and highly individual since C8, though Chinese influence has been noticeable during some periods. The language has appeared in several distinct styles. 'Colloquial' is fully Japanese, 'Epistolary' includes many Chinese words and expressions, 'Literary' shows distinct grammatical differences and in vocabulary is nearly two-thirds Chinese, while the 'Classical' style, formerly employed in all serious and philosophical writing was in fact a variant of ancient Classical Chinese.

Agglutinative structure, like Korean, unlike Chinese. Few consonants and vowels, most syllables open, *r* and *l* not distinguished from each other. Cases by means of post-positive particles. No true pronouns. Verbs all basically impersonal, with special negative forms. Adjectives verbal in form. Variety of honorifics distinguished. Numerals from 1 to 10 have two forms: from Chinese, *ichi ni san shi go roku schichi hachi ku jū*; native Japanese, *hitotsu futatsu mitsu yotsu itsutsu mutsu nanatsu yatsu kokonotsu tō*, 100 = *hyaku*. (Compare the former with Chinese).

Javanese

(MP/in) 18 m, central and east Java. Closely related to Malay, qv for description, with Sanskrit influence on vocabulary. Rich literature from C9.

Judaeo- LL

Judaeo-German (Jüdisch-deutsch) = Yiddish, qv.
Judaeo-Spanish = Ladino, qv.
See also Hebrew.

Jutish

D of Danish, qv.

K

Kafir°

(IE/ia.nw) 6 th speakers of a series of dialects in north west India, bordering on the Pamir mountains; including Kati (Bashgali), Veron (Prasun), Ashkun, Gawarbati, Phatura, Dameli.

Kalasha

(IE/ia.nw) Dialect of N.W. India, in Kafir° region but not belonging to that group.

Kalmyk, Kalmuk

D of Mongolian, qv.

Kamchadal (Itelmen)

(PS/ch) 800 speakers (in 1925), Koryak national region of north east Siberia and island of Shumshu. DD Sedanka (north), Khar'yuz (south). Influenced by Koryak and Russian.

Kanarese (Kannada)

= Canarese, qv.

Kanauji

D of Hindi, West, qv.

Karakalpak

(AL/tk) 186 th (in 1939) in Karakalpak national region and Uzbekistan. Roman alphabet introduced 1928, since when some literature based on northern form.

Karelian (Carelian)

(UR/fn.b/Fin) 370 th speakers (in 1926) of Karelian, and Olonecian on the east shores of lake Ladoga. Karelian is the official language (together with Russian) of the Karelian Autonomous Republic, but differs from Finnish only in some phonetic points and is better regarded as a dialect of that language. (Likewise Olonecian is better regarded as a dialect of Finnish than of Karelian). Strongly influenced by Russian. Written Karelian can be said to date only from about 1917.

Karen

(SN/tb) Apparently Sinitic language of southern Burma. Its more archaic dialects suggest relationship with Mon-Khmer.

Kartvelian (Karthvelian, Kharthvels)
= Georgian, qv.

Kashmiri
D of Dardic⁰, 1·5 m, Kashmir. Has become a literary medium, with additional elements from Sanskrit and influences from Persian.

Kashubian (Kassubian)
(IE/sv.w) 200 th speakers on left bank of lower Vistula, surrounded and dominated by Polish, to which it is related together with Slovincian, qv, in the Pomeranian sub-sub-group of the Lekhitic sub-group of western Slavonic—to give it its full title. Alternate Polish and German domination of the Kashubians throughout their history has resulted in strong influences from these languages. Treated as a regional vernacular, though publications of folklore, plays and radio programmes presented in it.

Katheravousa
= Greek (Modern), qv.

Kati
D of Kafir⁰, qv.

Kazakh
(AL/tk) 3·5 m (in 1959), Kazakh SSR. DD include Aral, not very fully investigated. Numerically one of the strongest Turkic languages of the Soviet Union, it possesses a literature dating back to feudal times, which became vigorous during C19 as the result of a revolt against Tsarist oppression and is still flourishing.

Khalkha
D of Mongolian, qv.

Khandesi⁰
(IE/ia.w) 233 th speakers of a series of dialects in the western part of central India.

Kharia

D of Bhili⁰, qv.

Khasi

(AS/mk?) 235 th speakers in western Assam of a dialect apparently transitional between Mon-Khmer and Munda language types.

Khmer

= Cambodian; see also Mon-Khmer languages.

Khoin (Khoisan)

(KH) The Khoin or 'Click' languages are spoken by about 60 th pygmies scattered over the wastes of south western Africa, comprising to the south Bushman (San), to the north Hottentot (Nama) and Berg-Dama, and the Sandawe and Hatsa languages to the east in Tanzania. These are grouped together (1) negatively, since they are non-Bantu and may represent indigenous languages prior to the Bantu migrations, and (2) positively, in that they are characterized by the possession of a series of consonants caused by implosions instead of explosions of air at the points of articulation. These are described as 'clicks' (the name Hottentot, given by the Dutch settlers, means 'stutterers'), of which Bushman has 7, Hatsa and Hottentot 4, and Sandawe 3.

Khowar

(IE/ie.nw) 7 th speakers of a dialect in N.W. India related to Kalasha and probably (less closely) to Kafir⁰.

Kirgiz (Kara-Kirgiz)

(AL/tk) 900 th (in 1959), Kirgiz SSR. Apparently one of the oldest (or oldest attested) Turkic tribes. Some close resemblances to Oirot. Formerly in Arabic script, Roman alphabet introduced since the Revolution. Literary and press publications increasing.

Kodagu

(DV) 40 th speakers of a Dravidian dialect in a small area of the mountainous region east of Mangalore.

Kohistani

D of Dardic⁰, qv.

Koine

= Greek (Ancient), qv.

Kola

= Kola Lappish, see Lappish.

Kolami

(DV) 29 th speakers of a minor Dravidian dialect in Gondwana.

Kolarian LL

= Munda LL, qv.

Korean

(KR) 38 m, Korea, some speakers in Manchuria, Siberia, Hawaii. DD: little difference between north and south forms, standard is that of former capital, Seoul. Origin and affinities unknown; agglutinative structure and other features suggest possible relation to Japanese, and of both to the Altaic languages.

History unknown before C15, though some indications of literature dating to C8AD. Originally written in Chinese characters, using some of the ideographs for phonetic values (as Japanese), but replaced in C15 by an alphabet called *On-mun*, consisting of basically phonetic signs combined into syllabic units. Literature expansive under C20 western influence, but the language is still not fully documented. Borrowings from Chinese, Japanese, Mongolian, Sanskrit and English.

Phonetically richer than Japanese, having 32 distinct

sounds. Accent of the spoken sentence indicates mood, e.g. affirmative, interrogative, dubitative, etc. Honorifics more elaborate than Japanese, varying for 1st, 2nd and 3rd persons. Decimal numeration: [hana tūl sēt nēt tasåt jǫsåt nilgop jǫdålp ahop jǫl]. No other numerals in true Korean, use being made of the hybrid Sino-Korean, based on Chinese.

Korwa
D of Bhili⁰, qv.

Koryak (Nymylan)
(PS/ch) 8 th (in 1936), northern part of Kamchatka peninsular including Koryak national area. Eight dialects. Reduced to writing by means of Roman alphabet in 1930, later replaced by Cyrillic. A modest literature has grown up in the Chauchuven dialect.

Kota
(DV) 1,150 speakers of a dying Dravidian tongue in an isolated patch in the mountainous region east of Mangalore.

Kui
(DV) 600 th speakers of a Dravidian language isolated from the rest of that group, in N.E. India, and receding to Oriya, the surrounding Indo-Aryan speech of the area.

Kumzari
D of Persian, qv.

Kuo-yü
= standard spoken Chinese, qv.

Kurdish⁰
(IE/ir.w) 5 m Kurds in Kurdestan and Zagros mountain region speaking a series of dialects related to Persian. DD: Gullī, Zhako, Barwārī, Amadiye, Zēbārī, Akre, Sheikhan, Sūrchī, Arbil, Rewandiz, Xōshnāw, Mukrī, Pīzhdar,

Bingird, Suleiman, Hewraman, Wārmāwa. Literature entirely oral, and no standard Kurdish language exists uniting these speeches. The major dialect is probably that of the town of Suleimanya, which shows signs of spreading northeast throughout the dialect range (together with its regional variant, Wārmāwa). Numerals (Suleiman & Wārmāwa DD): [jak du se čwār penỹ šaš ẖawt hašt nō da] 100 = [sad.] (Compare Persian).

Kurukh (Oraon)

(DV) 1 m speakers of a Dravidian tongue isolated in the Indo-Aryan-speaking area round the town of Abikapur to the west of Jamshedpur.

L

Ladin

see Rhetic LL. (≠ Ladino).

Ladino

= Judaeo-Spanish. A form of (archaic) Castilian (see Spanish) with Hebraic elements. Expelled from Spain towards the end of C15, the Jews spread eastwards. Today there are perhaps 100 th speakers in the Balkans and Near East, referring to their vernacular as Español (Spanish). Compare Yiddish.

Lahnda (West Punjabi)

(IE/ia.w) 8·5 m in N.W. India. Closely related to Punjabi proper, with some features associated with the contiguous Dardic dialects.

Lai (K'lai, Li, Loi, etc)

? (SN/th) 200 th in the mountainous central part of the island of Haiwan off the Chinese coast. Little known. Either a Sinitic language with strong Malayo-Polynesian influence, or vice-versa.

Lamajen
Subdialect of Minchia, see Chinese.

Lamut
D of Tungusic, qv.

Landsmål
= Norwegian, qv.

Lappish
(UR/fn.b) c 30 th: Norway 20 th, Sweden 7 th, Finland 2 th, rest in USSR (mainly Kola Peninsula). Many of these languages and dialects are spoken by nomadic tribes in remote regions and are therefore not very thoroughly classified. They are listed here as dialects of one language solely for convenience: DD (East group) Kola, Skolt, Inari; (North group) Inari mountain dialects, and those of Norwegian and Swedish Lapps as far as the next group; (South group) Ume, and Arjeplog forest dialects. These terms are all geographical. The people are called Lapps by the Swedes, Finns by the Norwegians, and Sa'am by themselves (Sa'am has also been used confusingly as an alternative for the dialect Kola Lappish).

A Uralian language regarded by some as a link between Finnish and Mordvinian. The Lapps have been in contact with Scandinavians from at least C6AD, and so have numerous ancient Scandinavian loan-words. Several written standards provided by non-Lapps mainly for religious texts: (1) of Finmark from C18; (2) of Herjedal (south group) from late C18; (3) of north group; (4) of Luleå. And, under Soviet encouragement, (5) of Kola Lappish from 1917.

Latgalian
D of Latvian, qv.

Latin*

(IE/it) Latin derives from one of a group of Indo-European dialects carried by invaders of the Italian peninsula at an early date. Praenestine or Archaic Latin was the dialect of the region of Latium before C7BC; other known dialects of the time include Faliscan (very similar to Latin), Oscan and Umbrian. With the growth of Rome, the *lingua latina* overcame and incorporated neighbouring dialects, thereby enriching itself and developing into the refined literary medium known as Classical Latin.

With the growth of the Roman State and the spread of the Empire Latin spread through Europe as the language of conquest, domination and then administration, in most cases resulting in the extinction of 'barbarian' languages—Etruscan in Italy, Iberian in Spain, Gaulish in Gaul. This was the spoken Latin of the Roman people, termed Vulgar Latin as distinct from the Classical tongue which in its refinement and conservatism remained the property of literators. Both colonists and colonized were considered to be citizens of Rome, and the conquering language referred to as *lingua romana*. For the development of this into Spanish, French, Rumanian, etc, see Romance LL.

The Classical language remained alive, inherited by the Church and retained to this day by Roman Catholics as the language of liturgy and theological learning. Ecclesiastical Latin is however a faulty continuation of the Classical, having undergone a period of transmission through the dark ages by priests whose mother tongue would be one of many 'impure' Romance vernaculars, while the pagan literature of ancient Rome was largely ignored. In liturgy and education Latin is pronounced on the Continent like modern Italian.

Despite the emergence of great literatures in early modern Romance languages towards the close of the Middle Ages, Latin continued to be used as the medium of more serious works—philosophical and scientific—throughout Europe until C15, establishing a tradition still to be found in the Latin titles of multilingual scientific publications of the present time.

Latin lives on in modern European languages as a source of vocabulary and roots for the creation of new expressions as the need arises in fields of progress of which the scientific is only one. It has also formed the basis of many international auxiliary, or artificial, languages.

Highly synthetic in structure. Noun has 3 genders, 6 cases reduced from 8. Adjective agrees; comparison by inflexion. Verb has four conjugations plus irregularities, 6 indicative and 4 subjunctive tenses by inflexion, increased by compound tenses and passive forms, 2 participles and 2 infinitival forms. Decimal numeration: unus duo tres quattuor quinque sex septem octo novem decem, 100 = centum. (Compare any Romance language; Greek, Sanskrit).

Latvian, (Lettish, Latviski)

(IE/bt) 2 m Latvia (Soviet Republic). DD: Latgalian (east, or Upper Latvian), Vidus (central), Tamnieku (west), Curian (spoken by a small bi-lingual fishing population on the Kurische Nehrung in E. Prussia).

Known in writing from C16, literature mainly modern. Slightly further evolved than its relative Lithuanian, though both represent an extremely archaic branch of Indo-European.

6 cases, significant tonality, complex verb system. Numerals: viens divi trīs četri pieci seši septiņi astoņi deviņi desmit, 100 = simts. (Compare Lithuanian).

Laz (Chan)

(CC.S) 160 th speakers of a Caucasian language, ranging from Batumi in Soviet territory (under 1 th speakers) along the coast of the Black Sea into Turkey. Having lost its cultural contacts with the main body of Caucasian languages, it has undergone profound influences from Turkish.

Lekhitic LL   *Sorbian (Wendish)*

(IE/sv.w) Branch of western Slavonic (qv) languages including Polish, Polabian[x], and a subdivision, Pomeranian, consisting of Kashubian and Slovincian, qqv.

Lettish

= Latvian, qv.

Lithuanian (Lietuvishkai)

(IE/bt) 3 m, Lithuanian SSR. Earliest written record is a catechism of 1574. Closely related to Latvian, qv, it is formally one of the most archaic Indo-European languages. Nouns have complex 7-case system, with singular, dual and plural; significant tonality. Numerals: vīenas dū trỹs keturī penkī šeši septynī aštuonī devynī dẽšimt, 100 = šimtas. (Compare Latvian, Latin, Sanskrit.)

Livonian

(UR/fn.b) 2 th (in 1939), a Fennic language closely related to Estonian but with Latvian word-loans, spoken in fewer than a dozen fishing villages on the Latvian coast. Giving way to Latvian. Known to have been far more extensive in Middle Ages.

Lolo

see Tibeto-Burnese LL.

Low German

Language = Plattdeutsch, qv. Languages = English, Frisian, Dutch, Flemish & Plattdeutsch, as distinct from the (High) German branch of western Germanic. The phonetic development (Second Sound Shift) which led to the distinction of German proper from the Low German dialects was completed by C6AD.

Ludian°

(UR/fn.b) 10 th speakers in region of Olonets (north east of Leningrad on shore of Lake Ladoga) of a series of patois, basically northern Vepsian but with influences of Carelian, and forming a transition between the two. Impregnated with Finnish and Russian.

Luoravetlan

= Chukchee, qv.

Luri

D of Persian, qv.

Lusatian

= Wendish, qv.

M

Macedonian

(IE/sv.s) 1·5 m in Macedonia, an autonomous region of Yugoslavia. DD: Western, in 2 varieties, of which the Central is the prevailing standard, South-western, South-eastern, Eastern and Northern.

Old Church Slavonic (see Slavonic LL) was, basically, the Macedonian variety of Old Bulgarian. Macedonia has formed part of the Bulgarian and Serbian states, the Byzantine Empire, and that of the Turks in C15. Expelled *who?* from the Balkans in 1912, the people were divided between Serbia, Bulgaria, Greece. Though basically a variety of Bulgarian (qv), transitional between it and Serbian, Macedonian was recognized as an official and literary language a year before the people were united in federal Yugoslavia (1944).

Like Bulgarian, it differs from other Slavonic languages in having shed many inflexions and become more analytic. Cyrillic alphabet, based on Serbian use. Numerals: *eden dva tri četiri pet šest sedum osum devet deset*, 100 = *sto*. (Compare Bulgarian, Russian, Polish).

(Macedonian refers also to an extinct language of that region: see Thraco-Phrygian[x] LL).

Magahi
D of Bihari, qv.

Magyar
= Hungarian, qv.

Maithili
D of Bihari, qv.

Maiya
D of Dardic[o], qv.

Makrani
D of Baluchi, qv.

Malagasy
(MP/in) 4 m speakers in the Malagasy Republic (Madagascar) of an Indonesian language related to Malay, qv for description. Several DD, standard is Merina.

Malay
(MP/in) 65 m. Its home territory is the north coast of Sumatra, and under the name *Bahasa Indonesia* it is the official language of that area. In addition it has become the most widely used language of commerce and general communications in the Pacific region, being spoken in the whole of the Malay peninsula, South China, Thailand, Indo-China, Straits Settlements, Java, Borneo etc. The Indonesian dialects of many of these islands are closely related to Malay (Javanese, Tagalog, Malagasy etc) which makes it easily assimilable to the islanders; Malay furthermore maintains its coherence through its simple structure and lack of significant dialects. In actual number of speakers it ranks high (about 10th) amongst the world's major languages.

Being one of the central Indonesian languages, Malay is

little removed from Old Indonesian by comparison with e.g. Malagasy (in Madagascar). Its vocabulary has been rather impoverished through extensive use by foreigners, but has benefited by many loans from Arabic, Persian and Sanskrit. Arabic evangelization in C13AD introduced Muhammedan culture including the Arabic alphabet, basis of the script called Javi which is still widely used. This is less suited to its sound system than the Roman alphabet, which is spreading in two varieties, English and Dutch romanization.

Its use as an official and commercial medium has eclipsed its more literary qualities. Malay folklore has been less studied than Javanese, and where for example the latter lends itself to poetic style Malay tends to the prosaic and rhetorical. Malay has provided many loan-words to European languages, e.g. cockatoo, gecko, gong, junk, ketchup, sago, orang-utang.

The success of Malay to date and its undoubted expansion in the future are largely due to the inherent simplicity of its nature: it is said to be the easiest to learn of all major languages. 5 pure vowels, few consonants and no awkward consonant clusters. Words basically disyllabic, and in root form not distinguishable as particular parts of speech. Construction by straightforward prefixes and suffixes of precise significance. Noun does not distinguish gender, number or case; verb does not formally distinguish tense, person or number, and has few irregularities. Rich in precise affixes to express shades of meaning, and in onomatopoeia. Copula (*to be*) not expressed; subordinate clauses rare; only minimum essentials expressed (i.e. as in 'telegraphese' style). Numerals (used with classifiers): satu dua tiga ĕmpat lima enam tujoh dĕlapan sĕmbilan sa-puloh, 100 = sa-ratus. (The symbol ĕ represents a glide-vowel between two consonants, and in speech is hardly distinguishable). See also Indonesian.

Malayalam

(DV) 17 m, a Dravidian language (no connection with Malay) spoken along the coast of Malabar, from the south-west to the tip of India. Earliest inscriptions C10AD.

Malayo-Polynesian (Austronesian)

(MP) The native languages of the Pacific area, chief representative Malay, and including Javanese, Hawaian, Tahitian and Maori. Some linguists have attached (in various combinations) such apparently distinct groups as PAPUAN, AUSTRALIAN, & TASMANIAN[x] to the Malayo-Polynesian languages in a broad group termed AUSTRO-ASIATIC, which includes the AUSTRO-ASIAN languages of southern Asia as well.

Each of the branches (see below) is fairly homogeneous, resemblances from language to language being marked; resemblances from group to group are less immediately obvious but nevertheless discernible. The main overall feature is that of simplicity (see Malay): simple sound-system, regularly disyllabic words, no noun declension, negligible verb conjugation.

MP/in: Indonesian (115 m) (Malay, Javanese, Tagalog, Malagasy etc);

/ml: Melanesian, i.e. Micronesian + Austrome-lanesian (1 m);

/pl: Polynesian (350 th) (Tahitian, Hawaian, Maori, etc).

Maltese

D of Arabic, qv.

Malto

(DV) 70 th speakers in Bhagalpur and surroundings, near border of India and East Pakistan, of a Dravidian language isolated in Indo-Aryan speaking territory.

Manchu (Manchurian)

(AL/tg) 200 th in scattered patches, N. China, all bi-lingual with Chinese. Known to have been in use C3BC in what is now Manchukuo.

Alone of the Tungusic LL (qv) it possesses a written literature, which reached great heights in C18 but was already giving way to Chinese in C19. Includes linguistic works and dictionaries of great value to modern linguists. The literature was given its initial impetus through the founding of the Chin Dynasty of China by the Manchurian chief Akuta, combined with the civilizing effect of the conquered country. The present Manchurian syllabery was derived from the Mongolian at the beginning of C17.

Mandarin (Kuan-hua)

D of Chinese, qv.

Mansi

= Vogul, qv.

Manx (Gaelic)

(IE/ct.g) Spoken by about a dozen elderly people in 1958, and used once a year in parliamentary ceremony. Common Gaelic (qv) was brought across from Ireland into Man and Scotland about CC4—5AD, Manx probably diverged from Scots (to which it is thus more similar) between CC13–15. Its early history and nature are imperfectly known—first written record is a translation of the Prayer-book about 1625, but since spelt according to rules of English ortho-graphy it is difficult to tell what sounds were intended. Being neither learnt nor propagated, it may be considered extinct. Numerals: un da tri kaire queig shey shiaght hoght nuy jeih. (Compare Irish).

Maori

(MP/pl) New Zealand, mainly in the North Island. Related to Samoan, Tongan, etc. See MALAYO-POLYNESIAN.

Marathi

(IE/ia.w) 20 m in Maharashtra area (western India, including Poohna, Goa, Bombay). Written records from C12; rich literature, especially poetry.

Marvari

D of Rajasthani, qv (IE/ia.w) 6 m speakers, N.W. Rajasthan.

Mazandarani

(IE/ir.w) A representative of the Caspian group of north western Iranian dialects; has been a literary medium since the Middle Ages.

Mazovian (Mazurian)

D of Polish, qv.

Melanesian

see MALAYO-POLYNESIAN.

Miao (Miao-tseu, Miao-yao, etc)

? (SN) or (AS). Several million speakers in tribes scattered through Chinese province of Kwei-Chou. Not known before C20, no literature, difficult to classify.

Micronesian LL

see MALAYO-POLYNESIAN.

Min (Fukien)

D of Chinese, qv.

Minchia

D of Chinese, qv.

Mingrelian (Megrel)

(CC.S) 242 th (in 1926), a Caucasian language spoken to the north east of the Black Sea. Literature only oral until recently.

Mirandês

D of Portuguese, qv.

Moldavian

(IE/rm.b) Strictly speaking, the northern variety of the
Daco-Rumanian dialect of Rumanian (qv). It occupies the
greater part of Bessarabia, which was ceded by Rumania to
USSR in 1940 and forms part of the Moldavian SSR. The
Soviet government has subsequently elevated the dialect to
the status of language.

Mongolian

(AL/mg) 3·5 m, official language, with Russian, of
Mongolian Peoples' Republic and Inner Mongolian Auto-
nomous Region. DD Khalkha, Buryat, Kalmyk (Mongolian
SSR), Mongol proper, or South Mongol (Inner Mongolia),
Aimak (some speakers in N.E. Tibet), Hazara (speakers in
Afghanistan). These are dialectal groups of patois, mostly
very similar and mutually intelligible.

Folklore and Buddhist literature from C13; modern
literature based mainly on Khalkha dialect in an alphabet
based on Cyrillic introduced 1941.

Regular vowel harmony as in most Altaic languages; but
less agglutinative in structure and showing some elements
of inflection. Variety of moods and tenses, but in most DD
person and number rarely expressed.

Mon-Khmer LL

(AS/mk) A series of languages scattered over Burma and
Indo-China, including:

(1) Cambodian (Khmer): 5 m, Cambodia;

(2) Talaing (Mon): 300 th, Burma—coast and inland
between Rangoon & Moulmein;

(3) Kasi: 235 th, isolated patch in western Assam, perhaps
transitional between Mon-Khmer and Munda LL;

(4) Palaung, Riang, Wa, etc: 175 th, N.E. Burma and on

Chinese border;

    (5) Nicobarese: 10 th;

    (6) Lawa, Kha, Bahnar, Pheng, etc.

Only Cambodian and Talaing endowed with much literature; records date back to CC7–8AD. Their respective alphabets derive from that of southern India, the Cambodian subsequently forming the basis of Siamese and Laotian scripts, Talaing those of Burmese and Chan. Both show linguistic and literary influence of Sanskrit and Pali (qqv).

Basically monosyllabic, much use of prefixes, but not suffixes. Numeration originally vigesimal (traces remain in Nicobarese), but now decimal. (See Cambodian).

Mordvinian (Mordovian)

(UR/fn.v) 1·2 m (in 1959), Mordvinian SSR. DD Moksha (south), Erzya (north)—fairly distinct from each other, each having its own literary standard. Loan words from Tartar and Russian. Newspapers in Mordvinian from 1920; much imaginative and technical literature. Cyrillic alphabet.

Munda (Kolarian) LL

(AS/md) 4·7 m speakers of related languages or dialects: Santāli, Mundāri and Ho tribes at the northern edge of the central Indian plateau; Betul district in central provinces (Kurku tribe); also the Sōrā and Gadabā, to the south of the main group. Remnant of a once more widespread language group ousted by Dravidian and Indo-Aryan LL, now decadent and obsolescent.

Rich in consonants, but no vowel or consonant clusters; little distinction between noun and verb; derivation by infixes; conjugation by suffixes; rich in verbal forms. Peculiar use of pronouns (*langue pronominalisée*): concrete nouns are expressed absolutely, while grammatical relations are achieved by suffixing to the verb pronouns which refer back (or forward) to the subject. (Thus, e.g. not *the village is small* but *the village—is-it small*). Numerals (Santali): [mit[s] bar pe pon more turui eae iral are gel] 100 = [more.isi].

Mundari
D of Bhili[o], qv.

Munji
D of Pamirian[o], qv.

N

Nahali
(NH) Spoken by a small group in the Nimar district of the Madhya Pradesh, Nahali was formerly assigned to the Munda languages but is now seen to be the lone representative of an unknown type distinct from other languages of India. Many loan-words from Dravidian LL and apparent structural influence from Munda.

Negidal
D of Tungusic, qv.

Negro-African
(NAF) A geographical term of convenience referring to the native languages of Africa south of the HAMITO-SEMITIC group. There is no justification for assuming NEGRO-AFRICAN to represent a linguistic unity.

Three groups have been traditionally distinguished:

(1) The KHOIN or 'Click' languages, which may or may not represent one distinct family (see entry);

(2) The Bantu languages, forming a coherent linguistic group (see entry);

(3) The remainder, ranging in a broad belt from the coast of Senegal to that of Kenya as a sort of buffer between HS and Bantu languages. These are referred to as Sudanic,

or Sudanese-Guinean, and have customarily been regarded as a family distinct from Bantu.

The term *Sudanic*, however, also appears to be merely geographically convenient, and the whole situation is complicated by the fact that western Sudanic languages show closer resemblances to Bantu than to the supposedly related eastern tongues, while others (e.g. Hausa) appear to have some connection with Hamitic if not actually forming part of that group.

The important languages are Hausa and Swahili, qqv.

Nepali
D of Pahiri⁰, qv.

Netherlandish
= Dutch, qv.

Norn^x
Dialectal descendant of Old Norse (see next entry) spoken in the Orkney and Shetland Islands until C17.

Norse (Old Norse)^x
(IE/gm.n) Replaced name *Danish* for the common Scandinavian language shortly before its split into the Eastern and Western varieties, which was complete by C10AD. Then referred to Western Scandinavian (Old Norse) in the Icelandic dialectal variety of which the greatest part of medieval Scandinavian literature was written (the Norse sagas). With the distinction of Norwegian from Icelandic and Faeroese, dating from C11, the term Old Norse drops out except in reference to Norn^x, see above. See also Scandinavian LL.

Norwegian (Norsk, Nynorsk, Samnorsk)
(IE/gm.n) 3·5 m, Norway. It would not be an exaggeration to state that there are several Norwegian languages. The original Norwegian stems from the Old Norse (see above)

spoken in Norway in later medieval times. The vernacular developed into regional variants while the literary standard remained largely synonymous with Old Norse. It was this diversity which led to the position of Danish as the official language of Norway under Danish rule from CC15–19, referred to as Dano-Norwegian, or Riksmål (= State language). In C19, the century of nationalism, a literary standard was formed from the original Norwegian dialects still spoken in isolated country regions: this is referred to as Landsmål (= the Country speech). Both varieties still exist, the Dano-Norwegian Riksmål now referred to as Bokmål (= Book or Literary language), the original Norwegian Landsmål as Nynorsk (= New or Neo-Norwegian). Although both languages are still in current usage, efforts are being made to adopt as standard an artificial combination of the two—referred to as Samnorsk (= Combined Norwegian). Thus Norwegian may be variously found under the names *Dano-Norwegian, Norsk, Nynorsk, Samnorsk, Riksmål, Bokmål* and *Landsmål*. In practice there is little confusion, however, since although Danish belongs strictly to the Eastern Scandinavian branch (together with Swedish), and true Norwegian (Nynorsk) to the Western, the two are mutually intelligible between educated speakers, together with Swedish. Numerals: en to tre fire fem seks sju åtte ni ti, hundre. (Compare Danish, Swedish, Icelandic).

Nynorsk
  = Norwegian, see above.

O

Occitan
  = Provençal, qv.

Oguz[x]

(AL/tk) Eleventh century ancestor of Turkish, Pecheneg, Kipchak, Turko-Bolgar.

Olonecian (Olonets)

Strictly, a dialect of Finnish; but see also Karelian.

Oraon

= Kurukh, qv.

Oriya

(IE/ia.e) 12 m, coast and inland of north east India, including towns of Raipur and Cuttack. Has a literary tradition of long standing.

Ormuri

D of Pamirian[o], qv.

Oroch

D of Tungusic, qv.

Oromi

= Galla, qv.

Osmanli

= Turkish, qv.

Ossete (Ossetic, Iron)

(IE/ir.o) 275 th, Ossetic autonomous region and part of Georgian territory in the Caucasus. DD: Iron (east, with two variants: Tagaur, which forms the basis of the literary language, and Tual to the south); Digor (west, at the basin of the River Urux). An Indo-European language isolated in Turkish and Georgian speaking surroundings, geographically midway between Slavonic and Iranian. Its position may be partly responsible for the peculiarities which formerly led it to be considered as a distinct branch of IE, but it is now seen as an aberrant member of the Iranian group (chief representative Persian).

Ostyak (Khanty)

(UR/ug) 18 th in the Khanti-Mansi national area of the Omsk province, western Siberia. 3 dialect groups, north, east and south. Some literature since 1931, Roman alphabet replaced by Cyrillic in 1937.

Ostyak Samoyed

see Samoyedic.

P

Pahiri⁰

(IE/ia.c) A group of Indo-Aryan dialects spoken in the mountainous north of India, the principal of which is Nepali, with 3 m speakers.

Palaeo-Siberian (Palaeo-Asiatic, Hyperborean)

(PS) The primitive languages of Siberia, though once more widespread, are now restricted to the extreme north east, and spoken by tribes following hunting, fishing and reindeer-keeping culture. Affinities with Eskimo and some other Amerindian LL suggest a distant relationship—Amerindians show mongoloid features and are assumed to have entered the New World from Asia across the Bering Straits. Palaeo-Siberian LL show in addition some phonetic similarities to Manchu and Mandarin. Inter-relationships not fully established, so classification uncertain. Ainu may prove to be Altaic, and Yenisei-Ostyak related to the Sinitic LL.

> PS/ch: Chukotian (ch.c Chukchee, ch.k Koryak, ch.i Kamchadal; qqv);
>
> /gl—Gilyak; /yk Yukaguir; /yo Yenisei Ostyak; /ai Ainu.

Pali*

(IE/ia) The religious language of Singhalese and Indo-Chinese Buddhism, dating from earlier than C1BC. It appears basically to be an Indo-Aryan language, but it is overlaid with borrowings which disguise its exact nature.

Pamirian°

(IE/ir.e) A dialect group in the Pamir mountainous region at the north east of Afghanistan, representing an early off-shoot of the eastern Iranian language and thus related to Pushto and more distantly to Persian. All are vernaculars with little or no written literature, and surrounded by Turkish, Indo-Aryan languages and Persian—the latter seems likely to oust them. DD include Shugni, Yazgulami, Ishkashimi, Sanglechi, Yidgha, Munji, Waxi, Ormuri, Parachi, Yagnabi.

Papuan

(PP) Native languages of most of New Guinea, of which it can be said that they belong neither to the MALAYO-POLYNESIAN nor to the AUSTRALIAN family. New Guinea is the largest island in the world and is not fully explored, and until further research has been carried out it cannot be stated that all the Papuan dialects are inter-related.

Parachi

D of Pamirian°, qv.

Pashai

(IE/ia.nw) An Indo-Aryan language or dialect spoken in the extreme north west of India.

Permian LL

(UR/fn.p) The Permian languages consist of Votyak and Zyryan°, and seem linguistically midway between Finnish and Hungarian. Next to Hungarian, known from C13, Zyryan is the oldest recorded Uralian language.

Permyak
D of Zyryan⁰, qv.

Persian (Farsi)
(IE/ir.w) 10 m, Iran, Afghanistan, Turkestan. DD Farsi
(the standard); closely related to it, Lūrī and Baxtiyārī
(south) and Kumzārī (Mazardam peninsula in Oman):
these three are non-literary vernaculars. Tajik, a simplified
form of the language spoken in Turkestan, uses Roman
script. Tātī, a hebraized variant spoken by Jews in Baku (to
the north west) and Apcherm peninsula, has peculiarities
of its own and is written in Arabic script. Also Gabrī,
peculiar to Zoroastrians of Yazd and Kirman; Sivendi in
parts of Fars; Balūchī, qv.

Old Persian CC6–4BC. Middle Persian known as Parsik
or Pahlavic (cf reference to 'Pehlevi' in Fitzgerald's
Rubáiyát, stanza 6), spoken by Parthians in Fars province
after collapse of Alexander's Empire in C3AD. Owing to its
political and cultural prominence this region saw the establishment of its dialect, Farsi, as the literary standard, C6AD.
Persian is written in a slightly modified Arabic script.
Numerous Arabic loan-words over the centuries (the
influence is still strong) now account for over 50% of the
vocabulary, and some grammatical alternatives, e.g. *house*
= *manzel* (from Arabic), plural *manâzel* (Arabic way) or
manzelhâ (true Persian).

Although Persian belongs to the eastern group of Indo-
European languages (qv), it reveals many startling similarities to the western, though some are coincidental. Thus
bad and *path* mean the same as their English counterparts,
and *mother* = *mâdar*, *brother* = *barâdar*, *daughter* =
dokhtar; *who* = *kî*, cf French *qui*; compare also *pedar* with
Latin *pater* (= *father*), *âb* with *aqua* (= water); and the
numerals. Considerable simplification of Indo-European
flexional system, word structure by regular affixes. No

gender, no article (except post-positive definite particle with direct objects), no case-system, two plural suffixes. Verb shows great degree of regularity; distinct present-cum-future and imperfect tenses, perfect and passive by composition. Copula *to be* (compare *ast* with Latin *est*, = *is*) has short form suffixed to nouns and pronouns. No formal distinction between adjective and adverb. Numerals: [jek do se čahar panj šeš haft hašt noh dah]. (Compare Hindi, Sanskrit).

Phatura

D of Kafir⁰, qv.

Pheng

see Mon-Khmer.

Plattdeutsch (Low German)

(IE/gm.w) Term denoting the fairly homogeneous regional vernaculars of northern Germany, linguistically distinct from German proper (High German). Plattdeutsch first appears with the poem *Heliand* (= Saviour), c830AD, referred to in this form as Old Saxon. From Old Saxon dialects are derived the Low German languages, Frisian and English. Although Plattdeutsch is also referred to simply as Low German, its speakers are bi-lingual with High German, and as the result of this strong influence over the centuries the former has lost many features relating it to the other Low German languages.

Polabianˣ

(IE/sv.w) Former Slavonic language of the Elbe ('Laba' in Polish) region, extinct since mid-C18. Known from vocabulary lists and short texts of c1700, which reveal similarities to Wendish, qv.

Polish (Polski)

(IE/sv.w) 30 m, Poland; 100 th speakers in Těshín district of Czechoslovakia; 3·5 m in N. America, 150 th

S. America, especially in Brazil. DD Mazovian or Mazurian (Mazovia, centre Warsaw), Posnanian (Wielkopolska, centre Poznań), Cracovian (Małopolska, centre Kraków), Ruthenian (Polish Silesia, centre Katowice; see also this entry since the name Ruthenian is doubly ambiguous). Kashubian, qv, is sometimes regarded as a dialect of Polish—it differs from the standard about as much as Scottish from the English —but will be found as a language entry.

List of Polish names in papal Bull of 1136; complete sentence in Polish occurs as a gloss in Latin document of 1270. Treatise on Polish orthography 1440. Earliest poetry C15. Printing introduced C16. Grammar begun 1778, Dictionary early C19. Growth of literary language during C19 period of Romanticism. Polish is the chief member of the western Slavonic LL (which include Czech, Slovak, Wendish), and has been open to heavy western European influence, especially French in the late C17; nevertheless it preserves some archaic features of Slavonic, including palatalization of consonants, and two nasal vowels.

Noun distinguishes 3 genders (m., f., neuter,) 6 cases (nom., acc., gen., dat., instr., loc.), 2 numbers (singular, plural). Verb in four main conjugations; perfective and imperfective aspects clearly marked, with iterative and semelfactive verbs included. Roman script. Numerals: jeden dwa trzy cztery pięć sześć siedem osiem dziewięć dziesięć, 100 = sto (cf. Church Slavonic, Russian).

Polynesian LL

see MALAYO-POLYNESIAN.

Pomeranian LL

= Kashubian and Slovencian, qqv. See also Slavonic LL.

Portuguese (Portughes, Português)

(IE/rm.h) 60 m. 9 m Portugal, 44 m Brazil. Also Goa (India), Macaw (S.E. China), Mozambique (Africa), Portu-

guese Guinea, Angola and islands off west African coast,
Portuguese Timor. DD: Estremenho, Alentejano, Algarvio
(south, including Lisbon), Beirão (central); Interamnese,
Trasmontano (north, respectively west and east). To these
may be attached Galician, qv, better regarded as a language
manquée than a Portuguese dialect; and Mirandês, spoken
in a very small region to the extreme east of Tras-os-
Montes, which is (or was) a cross between Galician/
Portuguese and Asturian/Leonese (DD of Spanish).

Origins: the Romance dialects (i.e. varieties of Vulgar
Latin) spoken in medieval Spain were very little differentiated, as a comparison of modern Portuguese, Spanish and
Catalan still reveals. The dialect of Galicia, in the north
west, is first recorded in 1192; the differences between
Portuguese and Galician did not appear before C14. The
Portuguese standard grew up around the city of Lisbon,
and was actively consolidated and made as different as
possible from Spanish in C16. The Galicians remained
within the Spanish-speaking orbit.

At first sight, Portuguese seems very similar to Spanish;
it underwent however considerably less influence from
Arabic. Its use of nasal vowels recals French, and in fact
the influence of French has always remained stronger than
that of Spanish.

Two genders, no case system, plural in *–s* or *–es*. Three
main verb conjugations; infinitive can be personalized.
Numerals: uma dous três quatro cinco seis sete oito nove
dèz, 100 = cem. (Cf Spanish, Latin, French).

Posnanian
D of Polish, qv.

Prakrit LL[x]
see Sanskrit★.

Prasun
D of Kafir[o], qv.

Provençal (Prouvenço, Occitan)

(IE/rm.g) 9·5 m over the southern half of France, most speakers bilingual with French. DD those of Provence, Languedoc, Auvergne, Limousin, Quercinol; that of Gascony differs considerably. See also Franco-Provençal°.

Origins: the Romance (qv) dialects of southern Gaul during the later period of the Roman Empire, characterized by *oc* = *yes* by contrast with the northern dialects having *oïl* (whence modern French *oui*), hence the regional terms *Languedoc* and *Languedoïl*, as well as the alternative name, Occitan, for Provençal. French, standardized from the Languedoïl dialect *Francien*, known from 842AD, Provençal from about 1000AD.

Both Provençal and Old French flourished as literary languages during the Middle Ages, Provençal reaching unparalleled heights: lyric poetry elaborating the theme of courtly love, developed by Provençal troubadors, provided inspiration and models for other Romance literatures (Catalan, Spanish, French, Italian), but, remaining unrivalled as the language of lyricism, it was learnt and regularly employed by foreign writers, especially poets, in preference to their own native Romance languages.

Provençal was thus one of the greatest languages of the Middle Ages. Its decline was precipitated in CC13–14 by papal suppression of heresies which originated in or gravitated towards the south of France (the pagan elements of lyric poetry proving in this respect somewhat of an embarrassment to the wellbeing of the language), and the subsequent encroachment of political and attendant linguistic hegemony from the north. Despite a revival during the nationalistic nineteenth century and an attempt to maintain a literary standard as a counter to the inevitable process of dialectal variation, Provençal has not achieved its former eminence; but it is still very far from dying out. Numerals: un doui tre catre sinc sièi sèt vuèce nòou dès, 100 = sèn.

Prussian[x] (properly, **Old Prussian**)

(IE/bt) An extinct Baltic (not Germanic) language related to Latvian and Lithuanian, spoken in east Prussia until C17AD. It is known from two vocabulary lists of C15 and C16, and some short religious texts of C16.

Punjabi

(IE/ia.c) 25 m speakers in Punjab including Lahore and Amritsar, major language of the Sikhs, and extending over India as far as the Chinese border. See also Indo-Aryan LL.

Pushto (Afghan)

(IE/ir.w) Official language of Afghanistan since 1936, population about 14 m of which one third speak it, Persian being widespread in the region. The language overspills its political boundaries into Persian and Indian territory. Turkish and Baluchi are also current.

R

Rajasthani[o]

(IE/ia.w) 18 m speakers of related dialects in Rajasthan region. Principal dialect is Mārvāri, to the north west.

Rheto-Romance (Rhetic) LL

(IE/rm.r) c 450 th speakers of three distinctive varieties of Romance, divided between Switzerland, Austria and Italy, a linguistic relic of the old Roman Province of Raetia (settled and romanized CC1–5AD). Once spoken perhaps as far north as the Danube, the Rhetic variety of Romance has been reduced by the pressure of German and Italian, and has survived only in the less accessible mountain regions. Though bearing similarities marking them off from other Romance languages—they seem midway between French and Italian—the three have never shared a common literary tradition. Friulan is numerically the strongest, but Rumansch has acquired the status of a standard language—

it was so recognized by the Swiss government in 1938 when Italian territorial claims seemed imminent on the possible fascist argument that it was a dialect of Italian.

(1) Rumansch (40 th), Swiss canton of Grisons: (i) Rhine Rumansch, Surselvan and Subselvan varieties separated by the Forest of Flims; (ii) Engadinish of the River Inn region, upper and lower varieties; (iii) a third variety is spoken further east in the Val Mustair. The Rumansch of the former Rhetic capital Coire (German Chür) gave way to Swiss German in C15.

(2) Ladin (12 th) of the Dolomites, valleys Avisio, Noce, Gadera, Gardena;

(3) Friulan (400 th) local speech of the Udine province, extreme north-east Italy. Once stretched as far as Trieste. Texts from end C13.

The name *Friulan* is fairly precise, but *Rumansch* and *Ladin* (obviously cognate with *Romance* and *Latin*) are virtually interchangeable. *Ladin* is sometimes found as a general term embracing all three varieties of Rhetic, but is apt to cause confusion by reference to *Ladino* (qv), which denotes Judaeo-Spanish and has no connection with Rhetic. Numerals (Friulan): un dói tre quatri cinc sîs sièt vòt nûf dîs, 100 = cent (Cf. French, Italian, Latin).

Riang
see Mon-Khmer LL.

Riksmål
= Norwegian, qv.

Romaic
= modern spoken Greek, qv.

Romance LL
(IE/rm) The Romance languages derive from the spoken or Vulgar Latin current as the major medium of com-

munication, administration and culture throughout the Roman Empire. As this venerable establishment declined and fell, linguistic usage became increasingly internal and provincial concerns resulting in dialectal disintegration, enforced by the 'substrata' of the previous regional languages such as Gaulish, Iberian etc and by the 'superstrata' of invading Germanic dialects. The name Latin, *lingua latina*, gave way early on to *lingua romana*, or *Romance* (cf *Romanz* in Old French, *Romans* in Portuguese, and the modern *Rumansch* language). The tradition of Latin proper was continued by the Catholic Church (see Latin, for the ecclesiastical variety). Not all Roman provinces lost their original speech, however: Greek, and Celtic British (see Brythonic LL), are two major examples of linguistic resistance, although the term *Romaic* for modern spoken Greek (qv) still bears witness to the former domination of a variety of Romance. No date can be put on the disintegration, in any case a very gradual activity, of Vulgar Latin or Common Romance, but it must have been actively on the course of change between C5 and C8AD. French proper may be said to date from the Strasbourg Oaths of 842 where it is recorded to our knowledge for the first time, and on similar grounds Italian is known from C8, Spanish, Catalan and Portuguese from C12, and Rumanian not before late C16 (which reflects a paucity of historical records rather than lateness of development).

The Romance languages can be grouped for convenience under the following geographic headings:

rm.g Gallic (French, Franco-Provençal°, Provençal)
rm.h Hispanic (Catalan, Spanish, Galician°, Portuguese)
rm.i Italic (Italian, Sardinian)
rm.r Rheto-Romance (Rumansch, Ladin, Friulan)
rm.d Dalmatian[x] (Vegliote, Ragusan)
rm.b Balkan (Rumanian)

The distinctive characteristics of these languages can be ascribed to various substrata and later influences: French to Gaulish and later Germanic, Rheto-Romance to Germanic, Hispanic to Iberian, with Spanish to perhaps Celtic and definitely later Arabic, and Rumanian to Slavonic. See also Etruscan[x] for possible slight influence on Italian.

Romany (Gypsy, Tsigane, Gitan, etc)

(IE/ia.r) Basically an Indo-aryan language spoken by perhaps a million Romanies spread over the Old World. Although Romany vocabulary remains fairly constant, the actual usage of the language in any particular group tends to reflect in grammar and idiom characteristics of the surrounding language of that area.

Rumanian (Român)

(IE/rm.b) 16 m, Rumania. Romance language with strong influence of Slavonic from C6 onwards, different types of Slavonic producing varying dialects of Rumanian. First texts from late C16, in Cyrillic script (Roman now in use).

DD (1) Daco-Rumanian (north): Valakian (basis of the literary language), Moldavian, q.v., (some speakers in Ukraine), Transylvanian.

(2) Macedo-Rumanian (or Arumanian), in Albania, Thessaly, Macedonia.

(3) Megleno-Rumanian: in a few villages in the valley of Meglena, north west of Salonika.

(4) Istro-Rumanian: Istria, south east of Trieste.

Two genders, which may be 'mixed' (change of gender with change of number), five cases, including vocative; enclitic definite article; verb has four conjugations, nine infinitives by composition, four tenses and three more by composition, four moods (including infinitive). Numerals: unu doi trei patru cinci sase sapte opt nouă zece, 100 = sută (cf Latin).

Rumansch
see Rheto-Romance.

Russian (Russkij)

(IE/sv.e) c 160 m (125 m native speakers), official language
USSR, the 'future world language of Socialism'. Also called
Great Russian by some who consider Byelo-Russian (White
Russian) and Ukrainian (Little Russian) to be dialects of a
larger 'Russian' language (which may also be found referred
to as Ruthenian, qv for correction). Though similar, these
three languages are distinct. Russian DD: North (five
varieties, and covering most of Asia following the spread of
Russian over the past century), South (three varieties in a
broad band running from Tula to Astrakhan, bounded on
west by Ukrainian); Central (in two varieties representing
a transition from North to South, and including Moscow
and hence the literary standard). Transitional dialects
appear between Central and Byelo-Russian, and South and
Byelo-Russian.

For origins, see Slavonic. Earliest written record of any
modern Slavonic language is that of early Eastern Slavonic
(i.e. forerunner of Russian, Ukrainian and Byelo-Russian),
Ostromir's *Evangelium* of 1056. The modern Russian
standard was fixed in C18, based on the Muscovite dialect
and finished on the model of the classical language, Church
Slavonic, which remains a constant source of enrich-
ment. It remains free from the influence of other
languages.

Although by the end of C19 speakers of Russian were
confined to Russia proper and numbered no more than 70
million, the extent of the language has increased enormously
with the formation of the USSR. It is employed as a second
language in all parts of the Union and is widely propagated
through the educational programmes of other states within
the Soviet sphere of influence. The increase is also of scope:

already boasting a rich literary tradition, Russian has proved itself capable of acting as a medium of scientific discourse and political philosophy, though the latter is somewhat belied by the tiresome, repetitive clichés directed to the West.

Russian is naturally becoming more widely spoken in the Union and shows signs of ousting minor languages such as those of the Samoyedic, Tungusic and Palaeo-Siberian groups, yet it is interesting that Soviet policy, while extending the major tongue as the medium of administration, actively encourages linguistic and cultural minorities from region to region, to the extent that some previously unwritten country vernaculars have during the course of this century acquired literary status. Whatever motives may be imputed to Soviet authorities for this encouragement, it contrasts very strongly with the attitudes of western countries, such as France and Spain, in respect of linguistic minorities.

The success of Russian as the 'future world language of Socialism' is not yet assured, though making some headway in eastern Europe. This may be largely due to the inherently archaic nature of the language itself: grammatically it retains complex declension and conjugation systems; phonetically it is rich in consonants and consonant clusters often difficult for foreigners to pronounce.

Written in Cyrillic. Noun has 3 genders, 6 cases (Nom. Acc. Gen. Dat. Instr. Prep.) and an occasional Vocative; no article. Verb has Pres. Past. Fut. and Conditional-cum-Subjunctive, two aspects (Perfective, Imperfective), four participles (Pres. and Past Active, also Passive), 2 gerunds (Pres. and Past). Verb *to be* acts as the only auxiliary, and as a copula is omitted. Numerals: *odin dva tri čjetyrje pjat' šjest' sjem' vosjem' djevjat' djesjat'*, 100 = *sto* (cf. Church Slavonic, Polish, Serbo-Croat).

Ruthenian
  (1) Language: see Ukrainian;
  (2) White Ruthenian: = Byelo-Russian, qv;
  (3) An alternative name for Russian;
  (4) A dialect of Polish, qv.

S

Saam
  = Kola Lappish, a dialect of Lappish, qv.

Saho
  (HS/cs.c) ? 40 th. A Cushitic language of Ethiopia, similar to Afar, but little studied and remaining a non-literary vernacular.

Samnorsk
  = Norwegian, qv.

Samoan
  (MP/pl) 65 th speakers in Samoa of a Polynesian language related to Tongan and Maori. Though bearing typically Polynesian features (largely similar to Malay, qv for description) Samoan has numerous loan-words from Arabic dating from C13.

Samoyedic LL
  (UR/sm) A distinct branch of URALIAN, which family includes Hungarian, Finnish and Lappish, the Samoyedic languages were formerly thought to form a separate family. Their speakers are of mongoloid type, and are thought to have acquired this speech through early contact with primitive Uralians. Present extension: east and north from the Gulf of Ob, into the Taimyr Peninsular, and spoken by about 20 th members of nomadic tribes.

The Northern language has three dialects: Yurak (Nenets) with Taiga and Tundra variants, Yenisei (Enets) and Tavgi (Nganasan). The Southern languages include Ostyak Samoyed (Sel'kup), and Kamassian. Other previously Samoyedic-speaking tribes known from C18 are variously extinct or now Turkic-speaking.

Though agglutinative in structure, Samoyedic shows slight tendency to flexion and traces of amorphism. Numerals (Ostyak): [ukkịr šitti nǟqịr tētti sombịla muktịt sel'či], 10 = [köt]. 8 and 9 are respectively 2 and 1 away from 10: [šitti t^{sj}äŋgitịl köt = 8]; 100 = [tot]. (Compare Finnish).

Sanglechi

D of Pamirian⁰, qv.

Sanskrit*

(IE/ia.nw) The language of the Vedic scripts (Rig-Veda, Atharoa-Veda, etc), of unknown age but reaching its classical period of maturity during the last few centuries BC: basically an Indo-aryan dialect from N.W. India, it was more or less fixed as a literary medium by grammarians, natably Panini during C4BC, and produced a great literature. As a literary language it is still used by Indian scholars, and, like Latin and Greek to the languages of Europe, it acts as a valuable stockpile of vocabulary and expressions still drawn upon by the modern Indo-aryan languages, notably Hindi.

Sanskrit means 'noble, perfect', thus terminologically opposed to the vernaculars or Prâkrits (= 'plebeian'), i.e. the contemporaneous Indo-aryan dialects which ultimately gave rise to the present-day languages of the region (see Indo-aryan). Eventually some of the Prâkrits themselves achieved literary status, modelled on Sanskrit, and from similar dialects grew up such predominantly religious languages as Pali^x.

Like Latin and Greek, Sanskrit is highly synthetic in structure, with three genders, three numbers, eight cases, and over 700 formal variations of the verb (cf Greek over 500, Latin over 140). Numerals: ēka dvā trī catúr páñca sâs saptā astā nâva dãça, 100 = çata. (Cf Hindi, Church Slavonic).

Santali
 D of Bhili°, qv.

Sardinian
 (IE/rm.i) 900 th in Sardinia speaking a language close to, but in some respects more archaic than, modern Italian. Besides a small colony of Catalan speakers, the Gallurese and Sassarese dialects of central Italian are also heard in the northern part of the island. The Sardinian dialects proper are Campidanese in the south, Lugodorese in the central area: the latter is the more archaic form, and in many respects is closer to early Roman Latin than any of the modern Italian dialects. Earliest record: Lugodorese between 1080 and 1085. As early as C13, this dialect appears to have been unintelligible to Italians.

Saxon[x]
 (IE/gm.w) The Saxon dialects represent a continuance of the Germanic languages after the phonetic breakaway and formation of early High German, which was effected by C6AD; they are the forerunners of modern Low German languages (Plattdeutsch, Frisian and English).
 (2) Old Saxon: 9th century precursor of Plattdeutsch, qv.
 (3) Anglo-Saxon: imprecise alternative term for Old English, see English.
 (4) West Saxon: the Wessex dialect of Old English, distinct until C14AD.

Scandinavian LL

(IE/gm.n) Swedish, Danish, Norwegian, Icelandic and
Faeroese. Swedish and Danish constitute the eastern branch
and are mutually intelligible between educated speakers;
Icelandic and Faeroese constitute the western branch and
may be mutually intelligible in print, if not in speech.
Norwegian has not fully decided which branch to belong
to—for its peculiar position and many aliases, see the
relevant entry. These together constitute the Northern
branch of the Germanic languages, and are thus related to
(High) German on one hand, and Dutch, English and other
Low German languages on the other. The oldest attested
forms of Germanic are of primitive Scandinavian type.

Primitive Scandinavian, as suggested by its own name
donsk tunga, appears to have originated in Denmark and
spread northwards, ousting the now extinct dialects of the
third branch, Eastern Germanic, first from Norway, then
from Sweden (for Eastern Germanic, see Gothic[x]). This
linguistic invasion was completed during CC4–6AD;
Gothic remnants are to be found in the regional name
Gotland (in Sweden) and probably as a substratum producing the peculiarities of the Gutnic dialect of Swedish
in that region.

The split between East and West Scandinavian occurred
during C10AD, the late Viking period, and a great body of
medieval literature was produced in the western form, Old
Norse, mainly in Iceland. Further differentiation into the
languages as we know them began about C11 and was
complete by C13, although the Scandinavian languages have
always remained very similar. In 1321 a canon of Uppsala
requested of the pope a form of penitential in the language
of the kingdoms of Sweden, Denmark and Norway,
since the various forms of speech were mutually intelligible.
Written Icelandic of the medieval sagas is readily
intelligible to modern Icelanders without special study.

Scots Gaelic (Gaidhlig)

(IE/ct.g) 81 th speakers in 1961, in some regions of the Highlands. Introduced from Ireland C5AD (see Gaelic LL), independent literature flourished around CC15–16. The language seems to have lasted less well than Irish, Welsh and Breton, the other living Celtic tongues. It is however at present being taught at all stages in schools in Skye, Inverness, and the outer Islands. Numerals: aon da tri ceithir coig se seachd ochd naoi deich, 100 = ciad. (Compare Irish, Welsh, Latin).

Scottish

As distinct from the Celtic Scots Gaelic, with which it should in no way be confused, Scottish denotes a dialect of English, exemplified in the works of Robert Burns.

Semitic LL

(HS) The major and more coherent side of the family HAMITO-SEMITIC, qv, and represented principally by Arabic, Hebrew and Amharic. The earliest known member is Akkadian, antedating 3000 BC, and current in the southern half of the Babylonian Empire till C5BC. It was eventually replaced by Aramaic, which also ousted Hebrew, but was in turn overcome by Arabic and is now fading away. South Arabic (distinct from Arabic) spread into Ethiopia from C3AD, displacing the once extensive non-Semitic Cushitic languages which still persist in small patches, in the form of Ge'ez^x which has since given rise to the modern Ethiopic languages, principally Amharic. Arabic, which must have been long current in Arabia though not recorded before C4AD, has spread over the whole of the Near East and throughout northern Africa, displacing non-Semitic languages now represented by Berber. Arabic remains the major Semitic language of the present day, and one of the great languages of civilization. South Arabic and Aramaic are disappearing, but Hebrew has seen a sudden revival in recent years. Nearly all known branches of Semitic have at some time proved important languages of civilization. (See individual entries).

Most of the typifying features of Semitic will be found in the description of Arabic. The principal characteristic is that of word construction on regular sequences of three consonants (tri-literal roots), denoting purely semantic concepts, grammatical modifications occurring as a function of intervening-vowel change. Thus the root *k-t-b* evokes the idea *write*—or, to follow the parallel more closely, *wr-t* —and by vowel insertion variously produces (Arabic) *kataba* = *he has written*, *ketebt* = *I wrote*, *el-kateb* = *writer*, *clerk*; (Hebrew) *koteb* = *writes*, *katub* = *written*, *ketab* = *the writing*, *script*.

Extinct Semitic languages include Akkadian, Ugaritic, Canaanite (closely related to Aramaic), Moabite, Phoenician (Punic) which spread from Israel to Carthaginian Africa before C5BC, Nabataean and Palmyrenian varieties of Aramaic, Syriac, Hurranian, Mandaean, ? Amorite, ? Sin-aitic.

Serbo-Croat (Serbian, Croatian[x]; Srp, Hrvat):

(IE/sv.s) 17 m in most of Yugoslavia, (Slovenia and Macedonia having distinct languages). The languages of former Serbia, Croatia, the Voivodina, Bosnia, Herzegovina, Dalmatia and Montenegro were mutually intelligible, so that their union in 1918 had at least a good linguistic basis. The Serbians are Greek orthodox, the Croatians Roman Catholic; the former write in Cyrillic, the latter in Roman script—otherwise, there is very little difference between their standards. DD: 3 distinguished and named after their respective words for 'what'. Shtokavian (*what = što*), is the basis of the literary standard, spoken over most of Yugoslavia and also found spoken in three villages of the province of Campobasso on the Adriatic coast of Italy; Chakavian (*what* = *ča*), in north Dalmatia and some Adriatic islands, with a more archaic accent and some differences in declension; Kaykavian (*what* = *kaj*), in north-west Croatia, forming a transition to Slovenian (qv).

For origins, see Slavonic LL. Known from C12 manuscripts. Some literature produced in Dalmatia during C15, particularly in Ragusa (now Dubrovnik), but literature mainly oral (folk ballads and stories), not written before C19. Grammar of 'Serbian' 1814, dictionary 1818; also known as 'Illyrian', and banned under that name by Austro-Hungarian authorities in 1843. Re-adopted by Yugoslav scholars in 1850, using central dialect, under the Vienna Literary Agreement. Numerals: jedan dva tri četiri pet šest sedam osam devet deset, 100 = sto (Compare Russian, Polish).

Shina

D of Dardic°, qv.

Shluh

D of Berber, qv.

Shugni

D of Pamirian°, qv.

Siamese

(SN/th) 6 m speakers in Thailand of one of the Thai LL, qv. Known in writing from end C13AD, using an alphabet based on Devanagari. Numerals: nung sang sam si ha hoh chet pět haû sip.

Sidama°

(HS/cs.s) A very loose and widespread series of Cushitic dialects, which together with Cushite proper (cs.c) make up a Hamitic branch in Ethiopia. They extend from 130 miles north west, to about the same distance south, of Lake Awasa. Information sketchy for statistics and classification. DD: (North) Gudello, Tambara, Alaba; (North-west to

East) Jamjam, Sidamo, Darasa; (South to West) Burshi, Konso, Gidole, Arbore, Gäläbä, etc; (West) Ometo, Dawaro, Gofa, Walamo, Abayo, Haruro, etc.

Sindhi

(IE/ia.w) 4 m, north west India. Its southern variety has become a literary medium.

Singhalese

(IE/ia.s) 4 m speakers of a rather aberrant form of Indo-aryan in the southern part of Ceylon.

Sinitic (Indo-Chinese, Sino-Tibetan)

(SN) An important series of languages over south east Asia, chief representatives Chinese, Siamese (Thai), and Tibetan. The fundamental relationship of these three branches is not fully worked out, though generally accepted. Less acceptable, through lack of sufficient information, is the grouping together of these with Mon-Khmer and Munda (herein referred to as AUSTRO-ASIAN, qv) in a larger INDO-CHINESE family. The difficulties of classification arise partly through incompleteness of studies and partly through the ideographic rather than phonetic nature of written Chinese. The exact relation of Miao and Annamese (qqv) to this and to the Austro-asian family is also undetermined: widespread reciprocal influences of the two major groups confuse the issue.

Several features are typical of the family as a whole, not all of which are fully demonstrable in every language and dialect, but which are fundamental to the character of each group. Three of the most obvious are as follows: (1) Mono-syllabism, i.e. the tendency is for each root to consist of a single syllable, which implies, since the languages are mainly analytic (lacking inflections), that the majority of complete words are monosyllabic. (2) Significant tonality, i.e. the meaning of any word may vary according to whether it is pronounced in a high or low tone, or a slide in either direction between the two. Some Chinese dialects have or had as many as eight distinct tones. Since there is a paucity of distinct sounds in these languages, and words are mono-syllabic, significant tonality becomes necessary to distinguish between numerous resulting homonyms. These two features affect the languages equally, and either may be seen as cause or effect of the other. (3) Use of classifiers with numerals. E.g. Chinese does not say *three pots* or *three wells*, but *three mouth pot*, *three mouth well*; not *three knives* or *three spoons*, but *three handle knife*, *three handle spoon*. (Compare English *a hundred head of cattle*, or *three rounds* (or *pieces*) *of toast* instead of *three toasts*).

> SN/ch: Chinese
> /tb: Tibeto-Burmese (Tibetan, Burmese, Lolo, Himalayan, Assam, Naga, Bodo, Kachin, Kuki-chin, Karen, etc)
> /th: Thai (Siamese, Laotian).

Skånsk ?

Aberrant D of Swedish, qv.

Slavonic LL

(IE/sv) In actual numbers of speakers, the most imposing of the Indo-European languages; chief representatives Russian, Polish, Bulgarian. The group as a whole shows some similariaties to Germanic and distinct relationships with Iranian. Closer similarities are to be found between Slavonic and the Baltic LL, with which they are often grouped together as Balto-Slavonic (but see Baltic LL).

No reliable records of Common Slavonic. Old Slavonic, spoken by the Slavs of Macedonia and known from the late C9, has characteristics relating it more closely to the modern southern branch (Bulgarian etc), and is also known as Old Slovenian or Old Bulgarian. Old Slavonic ecclesiastical texts probably not earlier than C11 reveal some local dialectal characteristics. Old Church Slavonic is the romanised form of O. Slavonic still used by the Orthodox Church. (See Church Slavonic).

Slavs appear on the historical scene CC5–6; oldest reference to Slavonic language CC5–7; first hereditary Slav states CC9–10. Written literature appears in C9 (O. Church Slavonic), mutually intelligible dialects of which were current over the whole Slav area. From C10 O. Slavonic produced three branches, later culminating in a series of distinct languages:

sv.e: (East) Russian, Byelo-Russian, Ukrainian;

sv.w: (West) Polish, Polabian[x], Kashubian, Slovincian (these collectively termed 'Lekhitic' as distinct from:) Czech, Slovak, Wendish (latter also called Sorbian, Lusatian);

sv.s: (South) Slovenian, Serbo-Croat, Macedonian, Bulgarian.

Phonetic characteristics: palatalization, pure consonants alternating with palatal variants; consonant clusters, no aspirated consonants, few true diphthongs. Grammar: highly inflective; verbal system distinguishes two 'aspects': perfective/imperfective (= completed/incomplete, or single/habitual). Syntax: word order fairly flexible owing to inflexions. For basic form of numerals, see Church Slavonic.

Slovak (Slovenský)

(IE/sv.w) 4 m in Slovakia, an autonomous part of Czechoslovakia. DD: Central (standard); Western, Eastern.

First traces found in Latin documents from Hungary, CC11–15. Czech was literary language of the Slovaks (the two being closer than at present), but Czech documents written by Slovaks show distinctive Slovak characteristics by C15. Introduced by Catholics into church books, CC17–18; Latin-Slovak dictionary 1777 followed by grammars. Central D was basis of Štúr's 1846 grammar, has since become literary standard. Official in Czechoslovakia since 1918. Roman script.

Phonetic system closer to that of O. Slavonic than other Slavonic LL, flexional system reduced. Numerals: jeden dva tri štyri pat, sest' sedem osem devät' desat, 100 = sto (cf Church Slavonic, Russian).

Slovenian (Slovenski)

(IE/sv.s) 1·5 m, Slovenian Peoples Republic (autonomous region of Yugoslavia) and in small adjacent areas of Italy and Austria. DD: 9 distinguishable, tending to remain distinct since the region is mountainous. Standard based on D of Dolęnjsko (Unterkrain), with the pure vowels of Goręnjsko D to the north.

Origins: distinct from the Serbo-Croat line of development since CC7–9, earliest mss (prayers and confessions, Latin script) probably C11. One of earliest recorded spoken Slavonic LL. People under German and Italian domination from earliest times, so main LL German, Italian, Latin have influenced the language, also Turkish to slight extent. Revived with Reformation C19. Grammar produced, late C18, translation of O. Testament same century. Modern era may be said to begin with poet Vôdnik (1758–1819). Movement in early C19 to use or combine with Serbo-Croat, but Slovenian in Roman script established c1839–46.

Preserves full declensional and conjugational system and regularly distinguishes dual number (elsewhere preserved in Slavonic only by Wendish). Numerals: èn dvà tri štiri pęt šęst sędem ǫsem devęt desęt, 100 = stǫ̂ (cf. Church Slavonic, Russian).

Slovincian

(IE/sv.w) Possibly extinct, spoken until the middle of this century by a few families in the parishes of Schmolsin and Grossgarde, Stołp region, north west Poland.

Somali

(HS/cs.c) 2 m, the most widespread of the Cushitic languages, spoken in Italian and British Somaliland, and between the two. Probably to be regarded as a dialect series.

Somian

= Fennic LL, qv.

Sorbian

= Wendish, qv.

South Arabic

(HS/sa) Few speakers of a Semitic language related to but distinct from Arabic, in one coastal patch between Oman and South Arabia, on Soqotra and neighbouring islands. Formerly extended over most of the coastal region of South Arabia; one form of it carried into Ethiopia in C3 (see Ge'ez). It may thus be said to live on in its Ethiopic descendants, but as a distinct language it is dying out.

Spanish (Español)

(IE/rm.h) 115 m speakers, of whom 30 m in Spain. Also official language of Mexico, Venezuela, Ecuador, Peru, Bolivia, Chile, Colombia, Argentina, Paraguay, Uruguay. Also either official or current in: Canary Islands, Rio de Oro, Spanish Guinea, Spanish Morocco; Canal Zone, Costa Rica, Guatemala, Honduras, Nicaragua, Panama, Salvador; Cuba, Dominican Rep., Puerto Rico; Philippine Islands. DD of Spanish proper: Asturian, Leonese, Aragonese (North, not including Galician, qv); Castilian (Central, the standard); Andalusian (South, somewhat aberrant, with stronger Arabic influence). For Judaeo-Spanish, see Ladino.

Origins: Vulgar Latin of the six Hispanic provinces of the Roman Enpire developed into several Romance (qv) dia-, lects from which later evolved Catalan, Galician-Portuguese and Spanish. The latter shows traces of an earlier Iberian (and Celtic) linguistic substratum, and the strong influence of Arabic as a result of the Saracen invasions of C8AD, reinforced by later Arabic borrowings by the learned classes.

Early records and development: Some religious texts in a recognizably Spanish variety of Romance from C10AD. *Poema del Cid* from C12, in Castilian dialect. Castilian became the major dialect and basis of the literary language from the latter part of C13, when the *Cronica General* was produced under the patronage of the Castilian Alfonso X. Since that time, Spanish has continued to play a major rôle in the history of European literature.

It has become since the days of discovery and colonization the fifth numerically largest language in the world in terms merely of actual speakers: in extent it is even more important, vying only with English and French. In particular, it has shown its genius in the field of trade and commerce, being widely employed both for that purpose and for general communication even between non-Spaniards and non-Latin Americans. This is very largely due to its phonetic simplicity and basic regularity of grammatical forms, making it easy for most foreigners to acquire. Numerals: uno dos tres cuatro cinco seis siete ocho neuve diez, 100 = ciento. (Compare Portuguese, French, Latin).

Sudanic LL

see NEGRO-AFRICAN.

Sumerian[x]

The oldest recorded language, known from pictographs dating to 3500BC, and from later records in cuneiform, which the Sumerians seem to have invented. The civilization extended from south of Babylon to the Persian Gulf; the language remained one of learning and culture after the conquest of Babylon. Cannot be related to any other known group. Numerals: *aš (geš), min eš limmu i(ia), aš imin ussu ilimmu u*, 100 = *geš. nimin.*

Suomi

= modern standard Finnish, qv.

Svan (Svanetian)

(CC.S) 13 th speakers of an aberrant type of Iverian language (see CAUCASIAN) in the higher valleys of the rivers Inguri and Tskenis.

Swahili (Kiswahili)

(NAF/Bantu) 8 m, spreading from its home region of Zanzibar and associated coastal strip at the expense of numerous other native tongues as the principal language of trade, commerce and general communication in East Africa. It possesses the most extensive vernacular literature of any of the Bantu languages, and a considerable body of poetry from C18. There is in addition a growing prose literature by native writers, and a large number of Swahili newspapers and magazines. Out of hundreds of native African languages, Swahili and Hausa (qv) are the most important and fastest thriving.

Swahili, being Bantu, is a predominantly Classificatory language. Nouns are grouped into nearly a dozen classes, each of which has a distinguishing prefix which must be attached to all nouns of that class and to any other words describing or otherwise associated with them. Thus, e.g., inanimate objects (including languages, see entry name above) belong to the *ki*-class, whence *kibanda kikubwa = large hut, kisiwa kikubwa = large island*. Plural objects are in the class *vi*: *vibabda vikunwa = large huts*. The prefix *m*-denotes persons: *mtu mkubwa = large man*. It will be noted from the above that the adjective *large*, whose basis is *–kubwa*, takes prefixes to make it agree with the class of noun it describes. Yet another class, prefix *u–*, produces nouns from adjectives: thus *ukubwa = largeness* or *size*. Numerals: moja mbili tatu nne tano sita saba nane tisa kumi, 100 = mia.

Swedish (Svenska)

(IE/gm.n) 8 m, Sweden and some coastal regions of Finland (Nyland, and the Åland islands and archipelago to the east of them). Comprises with Danish (the two are mutually intelligible to educated speakers) the eastern branch of Scandinavian, qv for further details. Amongst varieies of Swedish may be mentioned Gutnic or Gutnish, of Gotland, which seems to represent the influence of a Gothic substratum (Gothic was the language of Norway and Sweden when Scandinavian arrived from Denmark in C3AD), and Skånsk, a Dano-Swedish speech resulting from Danish rule of Skåna until 1676. Numerals: en två tre fyra fem sex sju åtta nio tio, hundra. (Compare Danish, Icelandic).

Syrian (Syro-Palestinian)

D of Arabic, qv.

Syryan, Syrian

= Zyryan, qv.

T

Tagalog

(MP/in) The official language (out of about three dozen) of the Philippine Islands; closely related to Malay, qv for general description.

Tahitian

(MP/pl) A Polynesian language (related to Samoan and Maori) spoken in the islets surrounding the main centre of the Society Islands, though losing ground in the administrative centre itself.

T'ai

= Thai, qv.

Tajik

see Persian.

Talaing

see Mon-Khmer LL.

Tamil (Tamoul)

(DV) 27 m, southern India (region of Madras), and north and east of Ceylon. The oldest representative of the Dravidian languages (qv) and boasting the richest literature. Inscriptions certainly from C5AD, possibly as early as C3, which make it, next to Sanskrit, the earliest attested language of the sub-continent. The standard originated in Madura. The first grammar traditionally dates from about C5, written by the semi-legendary Agastaya. Numerals: [or- ir- mu- nāl- ai- āR- ēl- en- toṇḍu pat-tu, 100 = nūRu].

Tartar (Tatar) LL:

(AL/tk) These languages, beyond being Turkic, do not in themselves represent a coherent or even distinctive group, since 'Tartar' is a name applied by many tribes to themselves. Volga Tartar has about 4 m speakers; also Crimean T. (Krymchak), Tyumen T., Tobol T., Ishim T., Irtysh T., etc.

Tasmanian[x]

Extinct since 1877, outcome of process of extermination of natives by colonists from 1825–30, which also accounts for lack of records. Thought to have borne possible relationship with AUSTRALIAN Aborigine, qv. Once five dialects. Numerals (N.E. dialect): mere = 1, pue = 2, above two became simply 'many'.

Tātī

D of Persian, qv.

Telugu

(DV) 33 m, numerically largest of Dravidian languages,

in south east India. A written grammar dates from C11, followed by Sanskrit-influenced literature.

Thai (T'ai)

(SN/th) 12 m, about equally divided between Siamese, Laotian and Vietnamese speakers. Other languages include Khamti, Tai-nai (Chan), Black and White Thai, Nung, Ahom extinct since C18 but still in use as a religious language, and possibly Lai (qv, which may however belong to the Tibeto-Burmese group). Annamese may also belong to this group.

These languages differ little amongst themselves, many being mutually intelligible. For general characteristics, see SINITIC, in which family they form a group related to Tibeto-Burmese and Chinese. All are in any case profoundly influenced from other sources, e.g. Chinese, Pali*, etc. (For Pali*, see Sanskrit).

All are written languages, but in varying scripts, such as Chinese ideographs, Burmese, Cambogian, etc. Siamese and Laotian boast literature from comparatively ancient times; the literary language of the Thais under Indian civilization was Pali*; and until recently Chinese was the literary medium of Annamese speakers.

Tibetan

(SN/tb) 6 m, Tibet. The standard literary language is based on the dialect called Balti. Known from C7AD, having the oldest literature amongst the Tibeto-Burmese languages; early works are mainly translations from Chinese and Sanskrit.

Tibetan shows some remarkable similarities to Chinese, which contrast with some equally remarkable divergences. Though fundamentally related, the two languages were not contiguous until recent times (C11AD), so the similarities may be as much due to coincidence and mutual borrowing from a third source as to vestiges of their common ancestor.

The language is rich in consonants, poor in vowels, with few diphthongs. Monosyllabism and significant tonality are marked features, in common with other Sinitic languages (qv for description). Numerals: [gčigs gɲis gsum bžiŋl a drug bdun brgjad dgu bču 100 = brgja].

Tibeto-Burmese LL

(SN/tb) 20 m speakers in S.E. Asia, chief representatives Tibetan and Burmese, qqv. Apart from these two, which have their own literature, most of the languages are unwritten. This group is related to Chinese and Thai in the SINITIC family and displays features which may be found briefly described under that heading.

(1) Tibetan;

(2) Burmese;

(3) Lolo, with DD Ahi, Agni, Lihu. (South west China around source of Red River);

(4) Himalayanº, DD Kanauri, Kanachi, Manchati, Chamba-lahuli (West, total 100 th speakers); Dhīmāl, Limbu, Vāyu (East, i.e. west of Bhutan, total 200 th);

(5) A series of DD lying between Burmese and Tibetan, including Bodo, Naga, Kachin, Kudi-chin.

(6) Karen (spoken to the south of Burmese as far as the coast west of Rangoon);

(7) Miao, possibly, though this may prove to be an Austro-Asian language.

Tigre

(HS/eo) About 170 th speakers in Eritreia, possibly amounting to 250 th by adding those of the Sudan. An Ethiopic (qv) language, with no written literature, spoken by a largely illiterate population, and losing ground to Arabic.

Tigriña

(HS/eo) 1 m, an Ethiopic language spoken in an area

between Axum and Massuwa (corresponding to the old Aksumite Empire). Overshadowed by Amharic, it has only recently acquired written form, which has made its way into the press but has so far produced only the rudiments of a literature.

Tocharian[x] (Tokharian)

Known from documents discovered early this century (1906) in Chinese Turkestan, revealing two varieties, Agnaean and Kuchean (formerly termed Tocharian A and B; Tocharian is a misnomer anyway). The texts seem to date from CC8–9AD, which suggests that it may have been still spoken by this late date. It is an interesting discovery, for, though contiguous with the Indo-aryan speaking area (eastern Indo-European languages), Tocharian shows some important features connecting it more closely with the western IE languages (Italic/Romance, Celtic, Germanic), a fact which upset some long-established notions about the history of INDO-EUROPEAN, qv.

Toda

(DV) Few hundred speakers of an obsolescent Dravidian dialect in the mountainous region east of Mangalore.

Tongan

(MP/pl) 30 th speakers in the Tonga Islands of a Polynesian language, thus related to Maori, Tahitian and Samoan.

Tosk

D of Albanian, qv.

Tsakonian

D of modern Greek, qv.

Tsigane

= Romany, qv.

Tuareg

(HS/bb) Dialect of Berber, qv. Perhaps 250 th speakers, scattered loosely over the Sahara in nomadic or oasis-dwelling tribes. The Tuareg area is roughly bounded by Timbuctu (S.W.), Zinder (S.E.) and the Ghat Oasis (N) (in the region of which, however, the dominant dialect is not Tuareg but Zenatian). Of the Tuareg dialects, only Tahaggart has been well studied.

Tulu

(DV) 650 th speakers of a Dravidian dialect related to Canara (qv) in the region of Mangalore, south west India.

Tungusic LL

(AL/tg) The minor native languages of a mongoloid people of primitive culture, appearing little in history apart from the Manchu fringe, one of whose chiefs (Akuta) founded a Chinese dynasty in 1115AD. They are spoken in Siberia and northern China, in an area bounded roughly by the rivers Yenisei-Omolon-Amur (west, east and south, respectively).

The Tungus proper (north) may number 300 th; their languages are more archaic and vigorous than those of the south (Manchurian). Tungus, as a major representative of the group, is richly agglutinative, with a full case and tense system. Related to the Turkic and Mongolian branches of ALTAIC, these languages exhibit the feature of vowel harmony, though to a lesser extent than in the other two branches. Tungus itself is particularly poor in vowel sounds.

Literature is confined to that of Manchu, qv. Most Tungusic dialects are now equipped with alphabets based on Cyrillic, which suit their phonetic character quite well.
DD North:

    tg.t: Tungus proper (Evenki), Orochon, Manegir,

Birar, Solon, Onkar;

tg.l: Lamut (Even), Orochel;

tg.n: Negidal;

DD South:

tg.m: Manchu;

tg.u: Ude (Udekhe), Oroch, Kyakar;

tg.g: Gold (Nanai), Olcha, Orok, Samagir, Kile; and others.

Turkic LL (Turanian)

(AL/tk) The Turkic languages form with Mongolian and Tungusic the ALTAIC family, and are its major branch. They extend in a broad belt across Asia from south west to north east, the extreme limits being from eastern Siberia to as far west as Macedonia in Europe.

The Turkic languages are difficult to arrange in any system of classification for two main reasons—homogeneity of language and heterogeneity of speakers. The Turkic-speaking peoples are scattered over a vast area, are largely nomadic, and even in recent history have been known to change languages completely from tribe to tribe; on the other hand, the language type, though far flung, is very stable and conservative, dialects and languages differing little amongst themselves. An extreme eastern member, Yakut, is quite distinctive, as is also an extreme western type, Chuvassian; but between them the people are too mixed to provide marked similarities and the dialects too stable to provide marked differences for the purpose of defining linguistic subdivisions.

The major language of culture and civilization is Turkish; entries will also be found for Chuvassian, Tartar dialects, Bashkir, Kazak, Karakalpak, Turkmene, Usbek, Kirgiz, Uigur and Yakut. (Arranged in this list from west to east, roughly).

Turkish (Türkçe)

(AL/tk) 26 m, the official language of Turkey. It is difficult to distinguish dialects of Turkish, since (1) Turkish itself may be seen as one of many little-differentiated dialects of a greater linguistic unity (see previous entry), and in any case (2) it is difficult to define and give a distinctive name to the Turkish of Turkey itself: in its broad sense 'Turkish' covers all those linguistic varieties referred to (above) as 'Turkic languages'.

Earliest records: C8AD epitaphs in Oguz, the precursor of modern Turkish. Medieval literature combines elements of both Western and Eastern cultures, particularly Arabic and Persian since the founding of the Ottoman Empire (1300AD), then French from C19. The language is written in a modified Roman alphabet of 29 characters, which has replaced Cyrillic, which replaced Arabic, which replaced Neo-Sogdian, which replaced a Turkish runic-type alphabet based on earlier Semitic (and so on: use has also been made of Manichaean, Syriac, Tibetan, Brahmi, Greek and Hebrew).

The major features of Turkish apply also to the Turkic languages generally and, in great measure, to the Altaic languages as a whole (i.e. including Mongolian and Tungusic). They are (1) Vowel harmony. In any word, which is basically monosyllabic but may be considerably extended by means of suffixes, a syllable containing a front vowel must be followed by a front vowel in any syllables added thereto, back vowels must be followed by back vowels, rounded vowels by rounded, and unrounded by unrounded. Thus, e.g. the plural of *ev* (*house*) is *evler*, of *öğretmen* is *öğretmenler* (teachers), but of *kulak* (*ear*) is *kulaklar*, of *baş* (*head*) is *başlar*. (2) Agglutinative structure. Word compounds are formed and grammatical processes indicated by the addition of suffixes to the root word; suffixes are regular in meaning and basic form, but have alternative vowels so as to conform with the vowel type of the root (e.g. plural *-ler* or *-lar* above). Example of word-building: *ev* (*house*)—*evler* (*houses*)—*evden* (*from the house*)—*evlerden* (from the houses)—*evim* (my house)—*evlerim* (my houses) *-evlerimden* (*from my houses*). Hence there are as many noun 'cases' as there are postpositions; prepositions are lacking. (3) No distinction of grammatical gender. (4) Plurality of little significance (no dual; singular used after numerals). (5) All roots are either verbal or substantival, and may appear in root form (producing respectively either an Imperative mood or Absolute case). Numerals: bir iki üç dört beş altı yedi sekiz dokuz on, 100 = yüz. (ç like *ch*, ş like *sh*; *ö* and *ü* as in German pronunciation; *I* and *i* represent a different sound from *İ* and *i*).

Turkmene (Turkmen, Turkoman)

(AL/tk) Under 1 m, Turkmenistan, Anatolia, Iran, Afghanistan. Considerable dialectal diversity, and the written language, standardized in C17, has not kept pace with the spoken. Originally Arabic script, replaced by a Roman script in 1927, now using a Cyrillic alphabet since 1940.

U

Ugrian LL

(UR/ug) Branch of the Uralian family, qv, comprising Hungarian, Vogul, and Ostyak. Of these, Hungarian is culturally and numerically the most important; Vogul and Ostyak are more primitive, and are spoken in an area from which the Uralians are thought originally to have dispersed. As a whole, the branch is more conservative than the related Fennic languages (Finnish, Estonian, etc).

Uigur (Uiguric)

(AL/tk) Spoken by Turkic tribes in the extreme west of

China. DD Taranchi (Ami region), Kashgar (Khotan region), Turfan (Lobnor region).

Ukrainian (Ukraïnskij; Ruthenian; Little Russian)

(IE/sv.e) 37 m (less than total pop. of Ukraine), others in minor groups in RSFSR, Rumania, and north east Slovakia. Some emigrated enclaves in USA and Canada. DD divided either into 3 (South, North, Carpathian) or 2 (Eastern, of Great or Dnieper Ukraine; Western, of Galicia). Standard: that of the Middle Dnieper region around Kiev (South or East Dialect).

Ukrainian represents a development, with Russian, from old Russian, both heavily influenced by Old Church Slavonic. Ukrainian characteristics discernible in mss. from Kiev region, C11, and Galicia, C12, but little differentiated from either Russian or Byelo-Russian during period of Lithuanian domination (see entry for Byelo-Russian). Flourishing literature from turn of C18–19. Linguistic struggle in C19: Bible translated, grammar published 1857, poetry by nationalist Shevchénko, but forbidden as language of instruction in schools, 1863, and in 1876 printing in Ukrainian banned throughout Russian Empire—officially termed 'the Little Russian dialect of Great Russian'. Ban lifted 1905. Ukrainian-Russian dictionary 1907.

Cyrillic script. Numerals: *odin dva tri čotiri p'jat' šist' sim visim devjat' desjat'*, 100 = *sto* (cf. Church Slavonic, Russian).

Uralian

(UR) Language family having as principal members Finnish and Hungarian, and also including Estonian and Lappish. Divided between three areas: Hungary, north east of the Baltic, and the Arctic coast of northern Siberia, including Yakutia.

The main branches are Fennic, Ugric, and Samoyedic; Finno-Ugrian may also be found as a family term before the relationship of Samoyedic was established. The features of vowel-harmony and agglutinative structure suggest a connection with ALTAIC (Turkic, etc), further reinforced by a similarity of phonetic features, of personal pronouns, and possibly other elements of vocabulary; for this reason, reference may occasionally be found to a URO-ALTAIC family, but such a coalition is not sufficiently demonstrable. Like HAMITO-SEMITIC, URALIAN possesses a few morphological features which some have taken to demonstrate a relationship with INDO-EUROPEAN; this is also beyond satisfactory demonstration, although the Finnish word for *a hundred* (*sata*) suggests a borrowing from Indo-European languages (cf Sanskrit *çata*), while, conversely, the English word *whale* suggests Uralian origin. Such borrowings do little more than affirm that the Uralian and Indo-European families have long been contiguous.

Other Uralian features besides those mentioned above include a general simplicity of verbal moods and tenses, lack of gender, and no formal distinction between noun and adjective.

UR/fn.b: Baltic Fennic (Finnish, Estonian, etc);
    fn.v: Volgan Fennic (Mordvinian, Cheremissian);
    fn.p: Permian (Zyryan, Votyak);
    fn.l: Lappish;
    ug.h: Ugrian (Hungarian);
    ug.o: Ob-Ugrian (Vogul, Ostyak);
    sm: Samoyedic.

Urdu

see Hindi (Hindustani).

Usbek:

(AL/tk) 5·4 m, Usbek SSR and Afghanistan, slight dialectal differentiation. Strongly influenced by Persian

(Tajik), and has lost feature of vowel-harmony. Literary language written in Arabic script until 1928, and Cyrillic replaced Roman in 1940.

V

Vegliote[x]
see Dalmatian[x] LL.

Vepsian (Chude)
(UR/fn.b) 31 th, 20 th Vepsians speaking the southern variety (Vepsian proper) on the south west shore of Lake Ladoga, 11 th Ludians speaking the northern variety consisting of a series of patois forming a transition between Vepsian and Vodian.

Veron
D of Kafir[o], qv.

Vodian (Votian, Votish, Vatya)
(UR/fn.b) 1 th in 1926, perhaps half that number today. Spoken in Kaprio and Kattila, small fishing villages near Luga estuary in Narva region of Leningrad province.

Vogul (Mansi)
(UR/ug.o) 6 th (in 1926), now perhaps 5 th, in Khanti-Mansi National area of Omsk province in western Siberia. Similar to Ostyak. Dialects variously enumerated at 7, 4, or 3. A literary language is based on the northern dialect. The first Vogul book was a translation of the Gospels in 1868, in Roman script. A primer dates from 1903. The establishment of a Vogul cultural base now seems to be favouring the growth of the language.

Volgan LL

(UR/fn.v) A branch of the Fennic languages, consisting of Mordvinian and Cheremissian.

Votyak (Votiak, Udmurt)

(UR/fn.p) 606 th (in 1939) speakers between the rivers Vyatka and Kama, mainly in the Udmurt Autonomous Republic. DD Vatka (north), Kalmez (south); little difference.

Known from a grammar of 1775. Cyrillic alphabet with diacritic marks introduced in 1905. First newspaper 1916. Vigorous literary activity since the Revolution have made it one of the richest minor languages of the Soviet Union.

W

Wa

see Mon-Khmer LL.

Waxi

D of Pamirian°, qv.

Welsh (Cymraeg)

(IE/ct.b) 656,002 speakers according to 1961 census, not counting children under three years. 99% bilingual with English. Phonetic and slight lexical differences between north and south varieties. Welsh speakers abroad tend to retain their language; there are small groups in USA and a well established settlement in Patagonia.

For origins and relationship with Cornish and Breton, see Celtic LL. Literature from C8AD, achieved great heights in the Middle Ages, especially in the realm of poetry. Despite the hegemony of English dating from a statute of 1536 attempting to prohibit the use of Welsh in

Wales, and the continuance of this dominance, it remains the liveliest of present-day Celtic languages, succeeding by nature where Irish has failed by force. The cultural tradition persists in the annual eisteddfodau, whose origins antedate C12 and which were re-established in 1819; programmes in Welsh are presented on radio and television; more modern literature is produced than publishers dare support; and there are some periodicals of a cultural nature, though no all-Welsh newspaper. A quarterly scientific journal, *Y Gwyddonydd* (*The Scientist*) was begun in 1964, using original articles and revealing a facility for turning the language to scientific use. Numerals: un dau tri pedwar pump chwech saith wyth naw deg, 100 = cant. (Compare Breton, Irish, Latin).

Wendish (Lusatian, Sorbian)

(IE/sv.w) 150 th on the Upper Spree (East Germany). DD Low Sorbian in Lower Lusatia, High Sorbian in Upper Lusatia; East Sorbian, in the region of Musau (Muzhakow) is probably extinct. Related to the extinct Polabian, belonging to the Lekhitic group of western Slavonic, which also includes Polish. Once considerably more widespread, forming a transition between Polish, Polabian[x], and Czech. Minor to German.

Since World War II, Wendish has been introduced into Lusatian schools. Numerous attempts throughout their history to achieve independance have always failed. Roman or Gothic script. Numerals: jedyn dwaj tři štyri pječ šesć sedm wosm dźesac, 100 = sto (cf. Church Slavonic, Russian).

Wen-li
= written Chinese, qv.

Worora
see AUSTRALIAN Aborigine.

Wu

D of Chinese, qv.

Y

Yagnabi

D of Pamirian°, qv.

Yakut (Sakha)

(AL/tk) 220 th (in 1926) of an isolated and archaic Turkic language. Written in Cyrillic script, replacing Roman.

Yazgulami

D of Pamirian°, qv.

Yenisei-Ostyak (Ket)

(PS/yo) 1·5 th (in 1926) speakers of the most westerly and isolated member of the Palaeo-Siberian languages. (≠ Ostyak, qv).

Yiddish (Jüdisch)

(IE/gm.w/German) Judaeo-German, or Jüdisch-Deutsch, derives from the Frankish dialect of High German spoken by the Jews in medieval Germany; it is much hebraized and contains elements of English, French and Polish. With the expulsion of the Jews from Germany dating from C14, it has ceased to be spoken there; its speakers are now so widely scattered that statistics are unavailable. East dialect (written in Hebrew characters) spread from Lithuania through Poland, Russia and part of Rumania, and represents the flourishing form of the language; the West dialect, of Alsace-Lorraine, is practically extinct.

Yidgha

D of Pamirian°, qv.

yoruba

Yukaguir (Odul)

(PS/yk) 500 (in 1926), in Yakutia, Siberia. DD of the Tundra and of the Upper Kolyma. Some educational works in the language have appeared since 1930.

Yurak (Nenets)

(UR/sm) 18 th (in 1926), from Kanin peninsular to estuary of the Yenisei. Best known of Samoyedic languages, and in many respects the most primitive.

Z

Zāzār⁰

(IE/ir.w) A group of dialects in western Iran, related to Persian, more closely to Gurani⁰, and contiguous with Kurdish⁰ which has considerably influenced some of the dialects.

Zyryan (Komi)

(UR/fn.p) Group of dialects which together with Votyak make up the Permian branch of the Fennic languages, (thus related to Finnish).

DD: Zyryan proper (North Zyryan), 10 varieties. The literary form, called Komi, is based on that of Syktyvkar;

Permyak (West Permyak, or South-west Zyryan), 2 main varieties, with a literary form based on that of Kudymkar.

Jazva (East Permyak, or South-east Zyryan).

I Brief Geographical Survey of Language Distribution

(1) *Europe*

The predominant languages are those of the INDO-EUROPEAN family, represented by the groups Germanic, Romance, Celtic, Baltic, Slavonic and the languages Albanian and Greek. Hungarian, in Central Europe, is an outlying member of the URALIAN languages, which are found mainly in the north: Estonian, Finnish, and the Lappish dialects form a contiguous group. To the extreme north-east, on the Russian littoral, other Uralian languages form a group which spreads into Asia—from west to east, Permian, Ugrian, and the Samoyedic languages. In south-west Europe, Basque remains the only representative of what may have been a pre-Indo-European family sometimes termed IBERIAN; in the Caucasus region to the extreme south-east, a multiplicity of languages and dialects constitute a NORTH CAUCASIAN and a SOUTH CAUCASIAN family, of which Georgian (SOUTH) is the most significant. Turkish also encroaches on European soil.

(2) *West, Central and Northern Asia*

Russian has spread its natural boundaries, and cuts through central Asia in a long strip reaching as far as the eastern shores around Vladivostok; in addition, it is the dominant language of civilization throughout the USSR. It is the only representative of INDO-EUROPEAN throughout this area. Other languages are those of the ALTAIC family, namely the Turkic, Mongolian and Tungusic groups. The Turkic languages differ little among themselves, although they range from Turkish in the west to Yakut as far north as the Taimyr Peninsular. The Tungusic languages lie north and east of Mongolian, covering most eastern regions of the USSR, except that east of the Koryak range and in the Kamchatka Peninsular are to be found archaic languages forming a PALAEO-SIBERIAN (or HYPERBOREAN) family, which shows some resemblances to native languages of North America.

(3) *South and Eastern Asia*

The PALAEOSIBERIAN languages may be represented by that of the Ainu tribes of the South Sakhalin. Neither KOREAN nor JAPANESE is demonstrably related to any other language group (or to each other), though both may have some connection with the ALTAIC family. The SINITIC family includes Chinese, Thai (including Siamese and Laotian), Burmese and Tibetan: Chinese has of course been a major language of civilization for nigh on four thousand years, while Tibetan, Burmese and Siamese are of considerable literary and historical interest. The rather heterogeneous AUSTRO-ASIAN family includes the Mon-Khmer group, of which only Cambodian (Khmer) is worthy of mention, possibly Annamese and possibly Cham—these are to be found in Indo-China, and the family is completed by the small group of Munda languages (principally Santali) in N.E. India. Andaman, in those islands, Nahali, in Central India, and Burushaski, in the Karakoram mountains of N.W. India, are further examples of linguistically isolated speeches, being unconnected with one another or with any known language group.

In southern India, the DRAVIDIAN languages (including Tamil, Telugu, Canarese) are probably the only languages indigenous to the sub-continent: many have long literary traditions. In northern India, the Indo-Aryan languages are representative of the INDO-EUROPEAN family. Like the

Dravidian family, the Indo-Aryan group consists of hundreds of distinctive dialects and languages—they include Hindustani, which is the official language of India since the recent relegation of English (still a *lingua franca*) to second place. Indo-Aryan includes also Punjabi, Bengali, Nepali, the Singhalese of Ceylon, and the geographically unbounded Romany language of the Gypsies.

INDO-EUROPEAN is also represented by the Iranian group: chief member Persian (in Iran); includes also Pushto (Afghan), Baluchi, the Kurdish and the Pamirian dialects (Ossete, spoken in the Caucasus, is also Iranian). Armenian, between the Black and the Caspian Seas, is an outlying member of the INDO-EUROPEAN family.

The Near East is the domain of the Semitic languages, principally Arabic and including also Hebrew. These belong to one branch of the HAMITO-SEMITIC family, which also extends into Africa.

(4) *Africa*

Arabic is widespread over the whole of northern and most of western Africa (Egypt, Libya, Tunisia, Algeria, Morocco, Mauritania). Other Semitic languages, dominated by Amharic, are spoken in Ethiopia. To the HAMITO-SEMITIC family belong the Berber languages spoken for the most part by desert nomads.

The Negro-African languages do not constitute one family, but consist of hundreds of languages and dialects, including a motley 'Sudanic' or 'Sudanese' group from Senegal to Kenya, a more homogeneous Bantu group south of an imaginary line from Cameroon to Kenya, and the KHOIN or Bushman-Hottentot languages of the south-west. Of the native languages both Swahili and Hausa act as *linguae francae*, culturally and commercially, over large areas. Of 'imposed' languages, English, French, Portuguese, Spanish, Italian and German are found in areas coincident with original colonized areas. Of greatest interest is Afrikaans, since 1925 the official language of South Africa: though basically a dialect of Dutch, its own standard differs from the Dutch standard, and, as such, it is the only Indo-European language to have taken independent root in African soil.

French is widespread in Malagasy (Madagascar), and some Bantu dialects are to be found on the north-west coast. The native languages are of the Indonesian group, which leads us to the Pacific area.

(5) *Pacific and Australia*

As languages of colonization, Dutch occupies the north-western half of New Guinea and most of the area to the north and west; English occupies the south-eastern half and the area east and south, including Australia and New Zealand.

Of native languages, the MALAYO-POLYNESIAN (or AUSTRONESIAN) family includes the groups Indonesian, Melanesian and Polynesian. One Indonesian language, Malay, has become an important medium of commerce and general communications.

The native languages of New Guinea are collectively referred to as PAPUAN, but may not all be inter-related. The Aboriginal AUSTRALIAN languages are still in existence. TASMANIAN is extinct.

(6) *America*

Modern languages of civilization: in the north, English (sometimes referred to as a whole as Anglo-American), with French in some parts of Canada, and Spanish in some parts of Nevada, Arizona and Texas. Spanish in Mexico, the central American 'bridge', and the western and southern countries of South America. Portuguese in Brazil. English in Guyana, Dutch in Surinam, French in French Guiana.

For the native languages, see entry AMERINDIAN.

II Languages of the United Nations

Afghanistan	Afghan (Pushto)—Persian
Albania	Albanian
Algeria	Arabic—French
Argentina	Spanish
Australia	English
Austria	German
Belgium	Flemish—French
Bolivia	Spanish
Brazil	Portuguese
Bulgaria	Bulgarian
Burma (Union of)	Burmese—Karen
Burundi	French—Flemish
Byelo-Russian SSR	Byelo-Russian
Cambodia	Cambodian (Khmer)—Laotian
Cameroon	French—Arabic
Canada	English—French
Central African Republic	French—Arabic
Ceylon	Singhalese—Tamil
Chad	Arabic—French
Chile	Spanish
China (Taiwan)	Chinese (Amoy dialect)
Colombia	Spanish
Congo (Brazzaville)	French
Congo (Leopoldville)	French—Flemish
Costa Rica	Spanish
Cuba	Spanish
Cyprus	Greek—Turkish
Czechoslovakia	Czech—Slovak
Dahomey	French
Denmark	Danish
Dominican Republic	Spanish

Ecuador	Spanish
El Salvador	Spanish
Ethiopia	Amharic—Arabic
Finland	Finnish—Swedish
France	French
Gabon	French—Arabic
Ghana	English
Greece	Greek
Guatemala	Spanish
Guinea	French
Guyana	English
Haiti	French
Honduras	Spanish
Hungary	Hungarian
Iceland	Icelandic
India	Hindustani—English
Iran	Persian—Arabic
Iraq	Arabic—Turkish
Ireland (Eire)	Irish Gaelic—English
Israel	Hebrew—Arabic
Italy	Italian
Ivory Coast	French
Jamaica	English
Japan	Japanese
Jordan	Arabic—English
Kenya	English—Swahili
Kuwait	Arabic
Laos	Cambodian (Khmer)—Laotian
Lebanon	Arabic—French—English
Liberia	English
Libya	Arabic
Luxembourg	German (Luxemburgish)
Malagasy Republic	French
Malawi	Portuguese, Bantu LL

Malaysia	Malay—Chinese—English
Mali	Arabic—French
Malta	Maltese—English
Mauritania	Arabic—French
Mexico	Spanish
Mongolia	Mongolian
Morocco	Arabic—French—Spanish
Nepal	Nepali—Tibetan
Netherlands	Dutch
New Zealand	English
Nicaragua	Spanish
Niger	French—Arabic
Nigeria	English—Arabic—Hausa
Norway	Norwegian
Pakistan	**W:** Punjabi—**E:** Bengali—Hindustani
Panama	Spanish
Paraguay	Spanish
Peru	Spanish
Philippines	English—Spanish
Poland	Polish
Portugal	Portuguese
Rumania	Rumanian
Rwanda	French—Flemish
Saudi Arabia	Arabic
Senegal	French—Arabic
Sierra Leone	English
Somali Republic	Somali—Italian—English—Arabic
South Africa	Afrikaans—English
Spain	Spanish
Sudan	Arabic—English
Sweden	Swedish
Syria	Arabic—Turkish
Tanzania	English—Swahili

Thailand	Siamese
Togo	French
Trinidad and Tobago	English
Tunisia	French—Arabic
Turkey	Turkish
Uganda	English
Ukrainian SSR	Ukrainian
UAR	Arabic
USSR	Russian
UK	English
USA	English
Uruguay	Spanish
Venezuela	Spanish
Voltaic Republic	French
Yemen	Arabic
Yugoslavia	Serbo-Croat—Slovenian—Macedonian
Zambia	English

III   Some Language Statistics

Not all countries which operate a national census ascertain the number of speakers of different languages, although, immigrants apart, very few countries are free from linguistic minority groups. Furthermore national and linguistic boundaries rarely coincide, so that even the known population of any given country is no more than a rough guide and usually forces an overestimate of the speakers of the major language.

Further difficulties arise in countries such as India where hundreds of languages and distinct dialects are spoken, and quite a few recognized as official, and in the case of languages such as Russian and Hindi, which are official over large multilingual areas. The greatest difficulty in seeking statistics is to be found in the case of languages such as English and French, which, through colonization, are spoken in many areas of the world, in some cases as official languages, in others as recognized secondary languages, and in others as the language of immigrants.

Finally, the problems of enumeration are increased by the fast growth of the population, especially in multilingual areas such as India and south east Asia generally. Figures quoted in the Dictionary are therefore rough estimates in many cases.

As far as these limitations allow, thirteen major languages stand out as being numerically significant: between them, they reach over half the world's total population. It is interesting to note the wide gap between the least of these and the numerically greatest of other languages, as well as the fact that all but four of them belong to the INDO-EUROPEAN family. Figures quoted are in millions:

(1) Chinese **750**, (2) English **300**, (3) Hindi **175**, (4) Russian **160**, (5) Spanish **115**, (6) Japanese **100**, (7) German **95**, (8) French **85**, (9) Arabic **75**, (10) Bengali, Italian and Malay about **65** each, (13) Portuguese **60**.

No other language appears to reach the forty million mark. There are strong grounds for assuming: Korean **38**, Ukrainian **37**, Polish **35** and Turkish **26**. For reasons suggested above, the languages of India are statistically dubious, but we may estimate: Tamil **37**, Telugu **36**, Bihari **35**, Punjabi **25**.

Languages with over ten million speakers each also include (roughly from highest to lowest): Rajasthani, Serbo-Croat, Malayalam, Rumanian, Gujerati, Hungarian, Dutch, Oriya, Greek, Czech. Four of these are Indian, and Dutch is a language of colonization, factors which present difficulties. To them may be added Javanese, Annamese, Hausa, Thai, Canarese, Burmese and Swahili.

IV   Language Guide to Europe

Albania
Albanian (see entry).

Andorra
The official language is Catalan, but French and Spanish are also in daily use. Most of the inhabitants are bi-lingual, many tri-lingual in varying degrees.

Austria
German; the Austrian dialect is distinctive, but not so different as to hinder the foreign speaker of standard German.

Balearic Islands
see Spain.

Belgium
Apart from German, spoken by about 500 thousand along the eastern borders of the country, the official languages are French and Flemish. The latter is spoken by over five million inhabitants in the north, the former by little over three million in the south. The inhabitants of Brussels and the surrounding district are for the most part bilingual, and number little over one million.

Bulgaria
Bulgarian is a Slavonic language and written in Cyrillic script, but not of the same group as Russian. Turkish is spoken along the Black Sea coast.

Channel Islands
English and French.

Corsica
Italian.

APPENDICES

Crete
see Greece.

Czechoslovakia
Czech in the west, Slovak in the east: little difference between the two, both are Slavonic languages but use Roman script. German is widely known as a second language.

Denmark
Standard Danish is sufficiently similar to Swedish to be mutually intelligible with it (see Swedish), but the Jutish dialect in the north is aberrant and may cause difficulty with the foreign speaker of Danish or Swedish. German is widely spoken, and English is reliable in the larger towns.

Eire
see Ireland.

Faeroe Islands
These constitute a Danish protectorate, and Danish is widely used. Faeroese is mutually unintelligible with Danish, being more similar to Icelandic, but few Faeroese are monoglot in their native language.

Finland
Finnish is quite distinct from the Scandinavian languages, though with many loan-words from them. Swedish is widely current as a second, and in some cases the only, language, especially in the coastal regions. Legally, both are official languages, but Finnish is the vernacular of 90% of the population. The influence of Swedish has been strong since the 12th century, perhaps earlier, and until the 18th century Finland was under the Swedish constitution. English and German are taught, and may be relied upon in large towns. Lappish is spoken mainly by nomadic tribes in the north.

France

As French is the only officially recognized language of the Republic, speakers of minor languages are for the most part bilingual. Breton, in the north-west, is closely related and similar to Welsh (and to the extinct Cornish), having been introduced from Britain in the 5th century. Flemish spreads into north east France from Belgium. Various dialects of Provençal (an important language during the Middle Ages) may be heard over most of the south, ranging from the Atlantic coast to the Italian border—including Limoges and Clermont-Férrand, but veering south of Lyon. Basque is spoken in the Western Pyrenees: it bears no relation to French or any other modern language, Roussillon (the Eastern Pyreenees) is the domain of Catalan, which, to the foreigner, sounds like Spanish and looks like a cross between Spanish and French. In fact it is transitional between Spanish and Provençal, and, like the latter, was an important literary and commercial medium during the Middle Ages. *Corsica?*

Germany (East, German Democratic Republic)

High German and Low German (Plattdeutsch). In Upper and Lower Lusatia is to be found the Slavonic language known variously as Lusatian, Sorbian or Wendish. Its speakers are bilingual with German.

Germany (West, German Federal Republic)

High and Low German, including dialects transitional to Flemish and Dutch. Most Germans use both their local dialect and the standard language. In Oldenburg are to be found perhaps a few hundred speakers of East Frisian.

Great Britain

99% of Welsh speakers are bilingual with English, but Welsh remains still the most vigorous of Celtic languages. The foreign speaker of text-book Welsh is advised to steer clear of North Walians, or to use English. Gaelic (Erse) is to be found in the west of Scotland and the outer isles, and is available on the school curriculum in Inverness and Skye. 99% of the few who do speak it are bilingual with English. (A Scandinavian language, Norn, was spoken in the Shetlands, Orkneys and extreme north of the mainland until as late as the 17th century—it has left many traces in the form of dialect words). In Northern Ireland, Irish Gaelic is confined to the west (Donegal). In Man, Manx Gaelic is just on, if not already beyond, the point of extinction. The language of Cornwall, allied to Welsh, became extinct in 1777, but has been exhumed by societies of enthusiasts. Everybody else speaks English, of one sort or another. The oft-quoted claim that the best English is spoken in Inverness is open to personal enquiry, should any reader care to carry out research.

Greece

A knowledge of Classical Greek is of slight help in the interpretation to some extent of written Katheravousa (standard literary Greek). From modern spoken Greek (Romaic) the dialects of the north and of Crete are somewhat divergent. Some Turkish, Bulgarian and Albanian may be found in border regions.

Holland

see Netherlands.

Hungary

Besides Hungarian, which is related to Finnish, German is widely spoken. Groups of Slovak and of Rumanian speakers are to be found.

Iceland

Icelandic. English is learnt and widely known as a second language.

Ireland

English throughout the island. In Northern Ireland, Irish Gaelic is only to be heard in some western regions. Irish is the official language of the Republic of Eire, but the majority of the population speaks English.

Italy

The standard dialect is Tuscan, based on the speech of Florence; other dialects are divergent even to the point of mutual unintelligibility. Linguistic minorities include speakers of German, Slovenian, Serbo-Croat and Friulan (for the latter, see entry 'Rhetic' languages). There are some speakers of Catalan both in Sardinia (north-west) and on the mainland. French is a good stand-by in the north.

Liechtenstein

German.

Luxembourg

The official language is *Luxemburgish*, a dialect of German (of the Franconian group, similar to Flemish), which is spoken by almost the entire population of about 320 thousand. Although technically a dialect, it has strong claim to language status since it is used for all official purposes, and the High German standard is used only in literature. French is also spoken.

Majorca, Minorca

see Spain.

Malta

English. Maltese is a distinctive Arabic dialect, written in Roman script.

Netherlands

Dutch. The inhabitants are notorious for their high standard of competence in English, French and German, especially English. West Frisian dialects are spoken on the mainland (Friesland) and West Frisian islands; its speakers are bilingual with Dutch.

Norway

The true historical Norwegian (Landsmål or country speech) differs from the State speech (Riksmål; or Bokmål 'book-speech'), which is a form of Danish (the official language under Danish rule from the 15th to the 19th centuries). Continual attempts to amalgamate the two have produced the form known as Nynorsk (New Norwegian). The speaker of Danish will have no difficulties, and Swedish will also be understood. German and English are not always to be relied upon. Those who wish to practise their Lappish are directed to the northern reaches of the Norwegian-Swedish border.

Poland

Polish is a Slavonic language, but of a different branch from Russian, and uses Roman script. Many speakers of German, Lithuanian, Byelo-Russian Ukrainian and Yiddish may be found.

Portugal

Portuguese is to a great extent mutually intelligible with Spanish. French has currency as a second language.

Rumania

Rumanian is related to French, Spanish, Italian etc, but has undergone so much Slavonic influence as to be generally unrecognizable to western Europeans as a Romance language. Hungarian and German speakers are to be found centrally (Transylvania).

Sardinia

Italian. Sardinian is a distinct but minor language. See also Italy.

Sicily

Italian.

Soviet Union

Russian is the major language both in theory and in practice, but it is Soviet policy to encourage the continuance of minor linguistic groups. These include Lappish, Estonian, Latvian and Lithuanian in the north west, as well as a standardized form of eastern Finnish, known as Karelian. Byelo-Russian and Ukrainian are closely related and similar to Russian. Georgian, a Caucasian language, flourishes in the Georgian SSR; Armenian, of the Armenian Republic, is a distinctive Indo-European language with a great literary tradition; Azerbaijani (Azerbaijani SSR) is very similar to Turkish. Moldavian, in that SSR, is accounted a language, though a dialect of Rumanian.

Spain

Spanish. Speakers of minor languages are for the most part bilingual, and include Basque in the north (Western Pyrenees and along the northern coast), Galician in the extreme north-west, Catalan in the east from the Pyrenees to Alicante, and in the Balearic Islands (Majorca, Minorca).

Sweden

Swedish is mutually intelligible with Danish and Norwegian, though Swedes sometimes say that a Dane sounds as if he is talking through a mouthful of porridge. The Skånsk dialect of Swedish, in the south, is basically Danish heavily overlaid with Swedish. The Gutnic or Gutnish language or dialect of Swedish spoken in Gotland is considerably divergent. Lappish is spoken in the north. German has some currency as a second language in Sweden, and is more reliable than English.

APPENDICES

Switzerland

The majority of Switzerland's 5½ million inhabitants speak German (*Schwyzertütsch*, a High Alemannic dialect): it is accounted for by three million speakers in nineteen of the twenty-five cantons. French is the major language of over one million inhabitants of Genève, Neuchatel, Fribourg, Valais and Vaud. Italian is spoken by most of the 200 thousand inhabitants of Ticino. Rumansch (see entry *Rhetic*), spoken in the Upper and the Lower Engadine (Graubünden), is also a recognized language.

under Italian it says 300th.

Turkey

That part of Turkey encroaching on European soil shares borders with Greece and Bulgaria, so that some Greek and Bulgarian are current as well as the major language, Turkish. Some French speakers may be found amongst a cultural élite, but as a last resort German is also reliable.

English?

USSR

see Soviet Union.

Yugoslavia

Principally Serbo-Croat and Slovenian.* German is current to some extent in the north. Minor groups include speakers of Bulgarian, Albanian, Hungarian, Italian, Rumanian and Turkish. Macedonian, in the south, represents historically an offshoot of Bulgarian.

* Acc. to his statistics, both Slovenian and Macedonian have 1.5 m. speakers. Why isn't the Macedonian also a 'principal' lg of Yugoslavia?

Sources and Acknowledgments

It would be impossible to mention every source of information—historical, cultural, ethnological as well as linguistic—which has been drawn upon in the compilation of this Dictionary, without appending a bibliography to most of the entries, which would add considerably to its length. Information on most of the languages included has come from monographs and works on individual languages and dialects. For groups of languages, however, the following should be mentioned: Meillet & Cohen (ed.) *Les Langues du Monde* (CNRS, 1952); Pei *The World's Chief Languages* (Allen & Unwin, 1961); Schmidt *Die Sprachfamilien und Sprachenkreise der Erde* (Heidelberg, 1926); Matthews *Languages of the USSR* (Camb. Univ. Pr., 1951); de Bray *Guide to the Slavonic Languages* (Dent, 1951); Melberg *Origins of the Scandinavian Nations and Languages* (Halden, Norway, 1951); Collinder *Comparative Grammar of the Uralic Languages* (Almqvist & Wiksell, Stockholm, 1960); Dumézil *Introduction à la Grammaire Comparative des Langues Caucasiennes du Nord* (Paris, 1933); Gray *Introduction to Semitic Comparative Linguistics* (Columbia Univ. Pr., 1934); Ullendorff *The Semitic Languages of Ethiopia* (Taylors Foreign Press 1955); Capell *A Linguistic Survey of the South West Pacific* (S.P.C. Tech. Paper No. 70). *The Great Languages*, a series of books edited by Professor Palmer and published by Faber & Faber, cover far more than the individual titles suggest, and much has been gathered from all that have so far been published. Illustrations and examples have been culled from individual works in the '*Teach Yourself*' language series, and from the later publications in Trubners 'Colloquial' Language series.

For initial encouragement and advice I should like to express my gratitude to Professor C. P. Magill of U.C.W.

ACKNOWLEDGMENTS

Aberystwyth, Professor C. E. Bazell of the School of Oriental and African Studies at London University, and to Mr. Leonard Cutts of the English Universities Press. Mr Robert Lord, author of '*Teach Yourself Comparative Linguistics*', was good enough to read through the typescript and to offer some valuable comments on some points of linguistic fact, and Mr David James enabled me to correct some errors on points of history and current affairs. I am indebted also to my brother, Mr Graham F. Parlett, for his assistance in transliteration and for the provision of notes on some of the more obscure languages which have found their way into this compilation.

In short, I have little to claim save indulgence for the errors which are bound to have slipped in while I was looking the other way.